Presented To:

_____

From:

_____

Date:

_____

Even When
Bad Things
Happen,

GOD
is
Good

Even When *Bad* Things Happen,

GOD is Good

Trusting in GOD When it Hurts the Most

DR. LEARY E. BONNETT, D.MIN

DESTINY IMAGE₀ PUBLISHERS, INC.

P.O. Box 310, Shippensburg, PA 17257-0310

"Promoting Inspired Lives."

This book and all other Destiny Image, Revival Press, MercyPlace, Fresh Bread, Destiny Image Fiction, and Treasure House books are available at Christian bookstores and distributors worldwide.

For a U.S. bookstore nearest you, call 1-800-722-6774.

For more information on foreign distributors, call 717-532-3040.

Reach us on the Internet: www.destinyimage.com.

ISBN 13 TP: 978-0-7684-4209-0

ISBN 13 Ebook: 978-0-7684-8737-4

For Worldwide Distribution, Printed in the U.S.A.

1 2 3 4 5 6 7 8 / 17 16 15 14 13

Dedicated to my beloved wife, Terry-Jan.

Acknowledgments

The birthing of this project ensued from the collaborative efforts of several midwives. Ms. Sherri Augustin played a pivotal role in ensuring that formatting aspects of the manuscript were adequately addressed before the final product went to print. During the completion of my doctoral dissertation at United Theological Seminary in Dayton, Ohio, Sherri also lent a helping hand in the completion of the dissertation. Thank you, Sherri!

In addition to Sherri's contribution, Rafael Reyes also provided invaluable computer expertise to the project. Further still, special kudos goes to my colleague in the Gospel ministry, the Reverend Kim Council, for her expert skills as a librarian, and who repeatedly provided me with clarification on cloudy issues. Special thanks also goes out to Dr. Mouyo Okeme for his efforts in proofreading the manuscript and recommending editorial changes that served to produce the best possible product.

Yet again, my deepest gratitude goes out to my pastor, colleague, and intellectual blood bank, the Rev. Dr. Arlee Griffin Jr., esteemed pastor of the historic Berean Baptist Church in Brooklyn, New

York, who afforded me the opportunity to sip from his homiletical saucer, and whose love of literature and stimulating discussions lit my candle and kept my literary wick burning high enough to complete this effort, which hopefully will be an invaluable source of inspiration to many who find themselves confronted with the difficulties of life.

Further still, my deepest sentiments go out to a loving family from which I remained cloistered in the third-floor office of our Brooklyn home for far too many hours during the two-plus years that I took to complete this project, and which I affectionately refer to as "The Upper Room."

Last, but certainly not least, my heartfelt gratitude goes out to the folks at Destiny Image Publishers, who demonstrated confidence in my writing abilities and gave me the opportunity to showcase this humble effort to the world community. Thank you, Destiny Image!

Endorsements

Even When Bad Things Happen, God is Good is theologically realistic, biblically grounded, Holy Spirit centered, full of psychological wisdom, and a very positive resource for addressing the lives of people facing tribulation. It is written, and speaks to the needs of the 21st-century Church.

Dr. Edward P. Wimberley
Professor of Pastoral Care
Interdenominational Theological Center
Atlanta, Georgia

Rev. Leary E. Bonnett has given us another gift. He has dared to accept the divine invitation to envision "what else" instead of surrendering to the deadening status quo of "what is." This wonderful book about trusting God during turbulent times will encourage you to open up your own life to the transformative power of God that continues to be at work in our world.

Dale T. Irvin
President and Professor of World Christianity
New York Theological Seminary

This book is a resource for churchmen and women who are ministering with members of congregations who are facing catastrophic events in their lives. Dr. Bonnett's book offers an opportunity for the Church to have dialogue around the biblical question of theodicy.

Eleanor Moody-Shepherd
New York Theological Seminary

Contents

Foreword

Believing that even when bad things happen, God is still good is a bitter pill for many people to swallow when they are impacted by adversity. And instead of turning hardship into worship like Job did, they shake their fists and rail at God for supposedly looking the other way, thereby allowing adversity to afflict them.

In this insightful treatise, the author draws on familiar biblical narratives to remind us that the onset of adversity need not bring our lives to a standstill—even though the pain that comes in tow with adverse circumstances is oftentimes so overwhelming that we are influenced into believing that life is over. However, in perilous times we must always entrust our circumstances to the providential care of our heavenly Father and never lose hope.

Trusting in God and never losing hope entails living with prophetic imagination when we are immersed in the floodwaters of adversity. It entails offering our brokenness to God so that He might plunge us beneath healing waters that bring us new life in the parched wilderness of our pain-predicament. It also entails opening ourselves up to the transformative source, who is God, of renewal and rebirth, that we might experience new life.

Anyone reading this book could expect to become emboldened on their faith journey by the insights provided by this outstanding biblical scholar, and someone I acknowledge as a beloved confidant and faithful colleague in the Gospel ministry. I am deeply and extremely appreciative of his indefatigable struggle in taking the time to compile such a marvelous and spirit-expanding treatise that is knitted together with insightful and uplifting words that bring hope to life's dark places.

Rev. Byron L. Benton, M.Div.
Associate Pastor, Berean Baptist Church
Brooklyn, New York

CHAPTER ONE

Life Is Sometimes Difficult

Humans dislike pain, and we tend to struggle with every atom of willpower to avoid becoming entrapped in its awful grip. On account of this inclination for self-preservation, no one voluntarily submits to adversity and the attending pain that bruises us at some point along this brief foot span of eternity's trail. But whether or not we are open to entertaining the likelihood of an encounter with adversity at some station on our pilgrim journey, it is an unsettling ingredient of human life. M. Scott Peck, M.D., concurs with this daunting reality, indicating that "life is difficult."[1]

The Issue of Theodicy

There is a persistent tension in the minds of people who experience difficulty reconciling the intersecting realities of a loving God, who allegedly has the welfare of creation at heart, with the existence of pain. The attempt to grasp both poles of this perplexing paradox gives birth to the issue of theodicy, which begs the question: Why would a loving God permit pain and suffering to disrupt the tranquility of His created universe? Not only are people aware of the ancient philosophical question in theology known as *theodicy*, but even individuals possessing scant acquaintance with biblical events are surprisingly familiar with stories that lend credence to the angst-ridden paradox, exemplified by the trials of Job (see the Book of Job) and the execution of John the Baptist in the synoptic Gospels (see Matt. 4:1-12; Mark 6:14-19; Luke 3:19-20; 9:7-9).

Job is the human face of biblical suffering, and someone referred to in literature as the quintessential wronged just man. The Old Testament narrative describes him as being God-fearing and extremely wealthy (see Job 1:1-2). In the ancient Middle East, the bottom line of an individual's financial portfolio was indexed by the acquisition of cattle, flocks, and family. In financial terms, Job could be likened to the Warren Buffet or Bill Gates of his day. But unknown to Job, he was cast as the leading man in a divine drama, in whose script God granted Satan liberal prerogatives to utilize His servant as a cosmic guinea pig. Before the setting of the sun on the dreadful and unforgettable day of Job's calamity, the ancient tycoon was subjected to an avalanche of adversity, beginning with the total loss of his vast financial empire, rapidly escalating in the death of his seven sons and three daughters. Job agonized under the enormity of the tragedy that assailed him. But despite the extremity of the suffering to which he was subjected, he maintained fidelity to God and responded to his pain-predicament with the solemn doxology: *"Naked came I out of my mother's womb, and naked shall I return thither: the Lord gave, and the Lord hath taken away; blessed be the name of the Lord"* (Job 1:21).

In the New Testament report, Herod Antipas, tetrarch (or governor) of Galilee and Perea, displayed the depth of his malevolence by imprisoning John the Baptist in the royal fortress at Machaerus, which was the southernmost stronghold, located five miles east of the Dead Sea in the rolling hills of present-day Jordan. It was in his execution chamber the locust-eating preacher was beheaded because he had the audacity to cross swords with the wife-stealing tetrarch. John unfortunately ignited the ire of Antipas by publicly denouncing the governor's marriage to Herodias, his half-brother Philip's wife. But even after Jesus was notified about John's incarceration within the confines of the massive desert fortress, and possessed the power to rescue His cousin and forerunner of His ministry from imminent death, He declined to intervene in the overheated public debate, thereby allowing the executioner's sword to sever the Baptist's head from his body.

Writing in *Rabbi Jesus*, Bruce Chilton reports that Antipas's first wife, daughter of Aretas, King of Nabatea, chose to abandon her husband rather than subject herself to the humiliation of a public divorce. In a skillfully choreographed display of antipathy toward her estranged husband, Antipas's wife gathered a group of loyal soldiers around her, and set out from the impressive fortress by camel, crossing the border into Nabatea—territory south of Damascus with its capital at Petra—safely returning to the domain of her father. John unfortunately injected himself into the firestorm of controversy, denouncing Antipas's marriage on the grounds that it violated a basic understanding of purity: martial intercourse with one's brother's wife was strictly prohibited by the Torah.

If Antipas's first wife's behavior proved to be a personal and political humiliation, John's attack on the governor's purity was a religious challenge with direct political implications: an illegitimate marriage implied that the ruler himself was illegitimate. No one needed reminding that the Herodians were Idumeans rather than Jews by origin. The Idumeans were forcibly converted to Judaism—and circumcision—during the rule of the Maccabean dynasty in 129 BCE, when the territories of Idumea and Samaria were annexed to Judea by the Hasmonean rulers in an attempt to strengthen and extend the borders of the Jewish nation. On account of this reality, any Herodian was an easy target of the charge of impurity. As such, Antipas felt the sting of the accusation that was leveled against him by John, who was a popular religious teacher whose ministry was located in the province of Judea. With his first wife safely out of the way, the imperious governor moved with lightning speed to make a public example of John, who dared to challenge the legitimacy of his reign. Unfortunately, John paid the ultimate price for his opposition to Antipas's behavior by having his head severed from his body. Fifteen years later, when Antipas suffered a crushing military defeat at the hands of his former father-in-law, Aretas, many Jews saw the humiliating event as retribution for his treatment of John. In his desperation to make an example of John, Antipas produced a martyr whose memory shadowed his inglorious reign.[2]

Antipas's rocky relationship with the Jewish nation was for all practical purposes a continuation of the legacy of his father, Herod the Great, who received from the Roman emperor Caesar Augustus the title "King of the Jews," on or about 31 BCE, after the emperor had consolidated absolute control in Rome. However, the Jewish people never recognized the so-called "King of the Jews" as being one of them, and they simply viewed him as a puppet of Rome. In lieu of the fact that the Jews lived each day with the expectation that the Roman occupiers would someday leave them alone and afford them the opportunity to chart their own destiny, they viewed Herod with some combination of smoldering resentment and hatred, and despised him intensely. Herod senior was well aware of Jewish sentiments toward him, and his insecurity compelled him to maintain foreign mercenaries and a secret network of informers among the conquered people. But despite his unpopularity as a leader, he still went to great lengths in the attempt to endear himself to his Jewish subjects, even to the extent of constructing an elaborate temple as a place of worship for them. Unfortunately, the populace was scandalized when he engaged in what their religious tradition viewed as an appalling abomination when he placed a Roman eagle—the symbol of Roman domination—above the gate of the opulent temple.

Both Job and John the Baptist recognized God as Sovereign Ruler over their life situation. However, despite the fact of having pledged their allegiance to the Creator, each was still impacted by adversity. For non-believers, the omnipotence of God becomes questionable when the two cases are referenced, because they cannot help but see themselves as being vulnerable to undeserved suffering, even if they chose to entrust their circumstances to the providential care of Almighty God. Skeptics would undoubtedly question: Why pledge allegiance to God if there is no guarantee that He will intervene in their life situation and safeguard them from adversity? Some people would argue that the existence of adversity is proof positive that there is no God, because if there were a God, adversity would be non-existent. This line of reasoning prompted Friedrich Nietzsche, the 19th-century German philosopher, to declare that "God is dead!"

Adherents of the Christian faith are intimately aware of the fact that God does on occasion allow painful events to ostensibly win the day. However, in those instances, when it is unclear what the divine plan might be, we are exhorted to trust Him. Percy C. Ainsworth, world renowned British clergyman and former pastor of Wesley Chapel in Birmingham, England, tells us: "We are to trust God not because we cannot trace Him, but that by trusting we may be able more to trace and see that God has a way through all these winding and crossing paths."[3] The apostle Paul provides followers of the Great Galilean with the comforting assurance of this reality in his epistle to the early church at Rome: *"And we know that **all** things work together for good to them that love God, to them who are the called according to His purpose"* (Rom. 8:28).

In the report of Job's encounter with adversity, Satan intimated to God that Job only ascribed worship to the Creator because He did good things for him. He wagered that if Job were to be subjected to bodily afflictions, he would abandon fidelity to God and curse the Creator to His face. Adding insult to injury as it pertained to Job's predicament, God surprisingly agreed to the wager by ratcheting up the stakes of the divine drama, thereby affording the Adversary free reign to lacerate Job's body with painful and putrefying sores that infested his frame from the crown of his head to the soles of his feet. However, despite the intense suffering to which he was subjected, Job remained faithful to a Creator who remained baffling, eerily silent, and inexplicable.

After receiving the report about Job's calamity, three of his close confidants—Eliphaz, Bildad, and Zophar—made their way to his hometown with the expressed purpose of consoling their beloved friend during his harrowing ordeal (see Job 2:11-13). However, instead of being sympathetic to Job's plight, the three judgmental men merely drove their oppressed brother into deeper despair. Voicing their misguided and offensive theology, the self-righteous trinity dredged up the familiar counsels of traditional wisdom about God's infliction of the wicked, and repeatedly accused him of having committed some grave sin against the Almighty, which in their estimation was the trigger event that opened the flood-gates of retribution against him. Knowing full well that he was innocent of any intentional sin against the Creator, Job denied any wrongdoing, and uttered the unswerving resolution: *"Though He slay me, yet will I trust Him"* (Job 13:15).

While he did yearn for the opportunity to plead his innocence before the Almighty in the heavenly court, at no time did he abdicate fidelity to the Creator, despite the torrents of adversity that relentlessly beat on his life's door. Job was eventually absolved of any wrongdoing by God, and the reward for remaining faithful to the Creator resulted in him being restored to full health from angry lesions that laid claim to his body, doubling of the riches that he initially lost, and the birth of seven sons and three daughters, whose beauty surpassed all the women in the East. Transformed by the ordeal to which he had been subjected, Job arrived at a deeper understanding of the goodness of the Almighty that prompted him to declare: *"I have heard of Thee by the hearing of the ear: but now mine eyes seeth Thee"* (Job 42:5).

In the case of John the Baptist, it might appear that Jesus's behavior bordered on callous indifference, in lieu of the fact that He maintained a hands-off posture during the firestorm of controversy that resulted in the Baptist's arrest and ghastly death of beheading at the hands of the executioners of the wife-stealer, Antipas. However, while it might signal an attitude of indifference on the part of Jesus toward the plight of His own flesh and blood, He always kept the objective of salvation at the epicenter of His worldview. A core principle of the Master's teaching indicates that death is merely a portal into eternity for those whose lives are entrusted to the providential care of our heavenly Father. So, while it might appear at first glance that John's predicament was ignored by Jesus, in addition to the Baptist being dealt a losing hand of cards from the deck of life, the ascetic rabbi actually received his eternal reward when he embarked on his exodus to the heavenly country. Scripture indicates that in God's economy, death is not a tragic event for believers, but merely the beginning of new life for those who entrust their circumstances to His providential care.

In his pastoral letter to the church at Thessalonica, chief seaport of Macedonia, Paul reminded believers at the fledgling Christian community of a core tenet of the Christian faith: *"But I would not have you to be ignorant, brethren, concerning them which are asleep, that ye sorrow not, even as others which have no hope. For if we believe that Jesus died and rose again, even so them which sleep in Jesus will God bring with Him"* (1 Thess. 4:13-15). Writing in *The City of God*, Augustine, the great North African theologian, saint, and former bishop of the North African coastal city of Hippo Regius, concurs with the Pauline admonition: "Death is not to be judged an evil which is the end of a good life; for death becomes evil only by the retribution which follows it. They, then, who are destined to die, need not be careful to inquire what death they are to die, but into what place death will usher them."[4]

Fallen People Living in a Fallen Place

The persistent question, "Why does God allow adversity to impact our lives?" is ancient. Throughout the long arc of human history, scores of inquiring minds have feverishly mined its endless veins. And no one will ever be able to fully comprehend the infinite mind of the Almighty, described by theologians as a "Holy Mystery" transcending any categorization. If we possessed the facility to fully plumb the depths of the Creator's thoughts, He would not be God, because God's thoughts are beyond the range of human understanding—unimaginably far beyond anything we could ever imagine.

Jesuit paleontologist, priest, and scholar, Pierre Teilhard de Chardin, indicates that God does not offer Himself to our finite beings as a thing all complete and ready to embrace. The Roman Catholic cleric argues that for us, He is eternal discovery and eternal growth. The more we think that we understand Him, the more He reveals Himself as otherwise. And the more we think we possess Him, the further He withdraws, drawing us into the depths of Himself.[5]

Despite the human inability to comprehend the infinite mind of God, adherents of the Christian faith subscribing to the doctrine of the Fall (see Gen. 2) believe that nature became corrupted when Adam and Eve disobeyed the Creator's prohibition to refrain from partaking of the fruit of the tree of knowledge of good and evil in the midst of the Garden of Eden. On account of our ancient ancestors' violation of the divine taboo, sin entered the world, unleashing in its wake an endless stream of adversity that continues to despoil creation since the occurrence of the rebellious act. On account of God's judgment against humanity, the apostle Paul concludes, *"We know that the whole creation has been groaning in labor pains until now"* (Rom. 8:22 NRSV). Theologian and philosopher, Paul Tillich, concurs with Paul's statement that by violating God's divine law, man destroyed the harmony of nature, and now there is enmity between man and nature, and between nature and nature.[6]

The world acclaimed British writer and theologian, C.S. Lewis, recognized as one of the intellectual giants of the 20th century, and arguably one of the most influential Christian scholars of his

day, posits the theory that our experience with evil is an indica-
tion that ours is a good world gone wrong, but still retains the
memory of what it ought to have been. Lewis argues that if evil
was something real, then there must be an absolute standard by
which it was known to be evil. He surmised that there must be an
absolute standard of good by which evil can be distinguished from
good. And his quest to establish such a gold standard compelled
him to conclude that this infinite reference point, this fixed point
above all personal and cultural bias, has its locus in God.[7] John G.
Stackhouse concurs with Lewis's sentiment: "Indeed, evil by definition marks a malfunction of the universe. Good probably has
to exist for there to be anything at all.... Indeed, something good
has to be there for evil to do something bad with it. Evil is always
derivative and thus not necessarily exist."[8]

The Lament Echoing Through History

At some place, and at some point in time, a scream goes out
from humanity toward the world, and ultimately toward the
Creator. This lament, repeatedly erupting throughout the Book of
Psalms, ensues from the pain welling up from the bowels of adversity in which we oftentimes find ourselves, and demands to know
why. The ancient poet laments the pain emanating from adversity,
just like Jesus and scores of suffering souls who were subjected to
the crush of its hammer blow: *My God, my God, why hast Thou
forsaken me? Why art Thou so far from helping me, and from the
words of my roaring?"* (Ps. 22:1).

Each generation screams to God from its own moment in the
attempt to discover meaning within its age and cultural assumptions. We scream, because at the core of our being we recognize

that the arena of suffering is not our natural habitat. This recognition has spawned a booming market of therapeutic agents that compete with each other for recognition as the perfect palliative for human suffering. As we search for panaceas to cope with the pain that we experience deep on the inside, we employ an extensive menu of chemical aids and stimulants. In our post-modern world, pharmaceutical companies are exalted by millions of suffering souls as shrines of healing in the ongoing battle against the vast array of maladies that threaten to degrade our sense of well-being. But even though we might obtain temporary solace in the wonder-working efficacy of miracle drugs, we recognize that ultimately we need help from something more reliable than opiates and sedatives in order to successfully navigate life's strenuous journey. We need God—God's self.

There Is a Pathway Leading Out of Suffering

Scripture puts us on notice that suffering is a painful hurdle which each soul is compelled to navigate at some station on our pilgrim journey. However, it informs us that the hardships of life need never be final or ultimate. Jesus allayed the anxieties of His disciples with the comforting affirmation, informing them that even though they would be impacted by the storm forces of adversity, He is still Lord over *all* of life's circumstances (see John 16:33). The consoling words of the Master indicate that there is a pathway emerging from life's difficult arenas when we entrust our circumstances to the providential care of Almighty God.

While our Lord's exhortation in no way attempts to ignore the reality of suffering by casually sweeping it under the rug, it signifies that the spark of life need never be extinguished with the onset of adversity. His exhortation additionally indicates that when we afford the Almighty final say over our life circumstances, we are at no time at the complete mercy of forces outside of ourselves. As such, adversity will never be a life sentence that culminates in self-diminishment. This is true because the gift of God's availing grace imbues our perspective with the kind of hope that enables us to visualize possibilities with our spiritual eyes that we are unable to envision with our physical eyes.

The pathway of pain preceded the advent of modern-day therapeutic programs; and down through the centuries, scores of individuals were compelled to navigate the ancient roadway whose essentials have been traversed and proven reliable by prophets and common run-of-the-mill folk who struggled for the very survival of their spirit in the crucible of adversity. Surprisingly, the pain-drenched highway has been traversed by the Author of Life Himself, who has gone before, who knows the way, and whose legacy left an indelible trail of spiritual footprints for humanity to follow. And unique to this highway is God's eternal promise flashing across the centuries, providing us with the assurance that He will never leave us nor forsake us (see Heb. 13:5). While we will be subjected to turbulent experiences along this brief and oftentimes perilous stretch of eternity, the pain and agony embroidering its trying and twisting turns is by no means the final destination of humanity.

Saint Augustine informs us that the soul's true destination is the "City of God." The 4th-century Church leader embraced the biblical truth that heaven is the eternal home of humanity, and points to an all-encompassing power in the universe far more powerful than any difficulty that might assail us on this side of glory.[9] Armed with this steadying assurance, a long line of sufferers who trekked across the sands of time recognized the wisdom of hitching their destiny on the promises enshrined in God's word. The great cloud of witnesses recognized that not only would the Creator avail them strength to battle the headwinds of adversity, He would also endow them with power to transcend its crippling effects and render them the recipients of abundant life.

In the grand scheme of things, the quality of an individual's life is not contingent on the presence or absence of the difficulties that assail them during their earthly pilgrimage. It is about recognizing the immanence of the Almighty insinuated in life's troubling circumstances. Spiritual writer Richard J. Foster states, "God's activity permeates all things, even the most trivial."[10] And David G. Benner concurs with Foster's statement, writing that, "God interpenetrates every part of creation, and nothing exists in creation that is independent of God."[11]

Life Has Meaning, Even During the Onset of Difficult Times

Since the sum total of our existence is not defined by the presence or absence of difficulties, our lives continue to have meaning and count for something in the amazing drama of the great human story, even when difficulties of the worst kind assail us. Scores of individuals that were subjected to painful ordeals provided the world with "grounding" testimonials about being the recipients of healing from a source that lay beyond the range of their limited capabilities—from beyond the material universe.

A few days after receiving her high school diploma at Woodlawn Senior High School in suburban Baltimore, Maryland,

Joni Eareckson Tada was paralyzed in a diving accident in Chesapeake Bay. She struck her head at the bottom of a shallow part of the bay, resulting in a fracture dislocation of the spinal column at the fourth and fifth cervical level. The accident completely severed her spinal cord and rendered her a quadriplegic. After experiencing the life-changing tragedy, the determination to anchor her providence on the promises enshrined in God's word enabled the 17-year-old to battle through spells of depression and frustration, and eventually established her as an icon of hope to millions of suffering people the world over. Her highly acclaimed artwork, which is painstakingly accomplished by holding paintbrushes in her teeth, her public speaking, television interviews, her autobiographical book *Joni*, and a highly acclaimed motion picture chronicling her inspirational life experiences, deposited her on the public stage, which she skillfully utilizes as a platform to highlight the awful plight of suffering humanity.[12]

After being assailed by tragedy that irrevocably altered the landscape of her life, Joni was presented with the choice of crawling into a shell, where she could have spent the remaining days of her life immersed in a state of self-indulgent gloom, or courageously moving forward in faith to live life as full as she possibly could under the circumstances. Fortunately, she settled on the latter option. Instead of allowing self-pity the opportunity to set up camp within the precincts of her spirit, shrink her world, sabotage her future, and limit her horizons, she drilled deep into the reservoir of faith and hope, percolating at the core of her being, employing them as agents of transformation that enabled her to live life to the fullest extent possible. Confronted by seemingly insurmountable odds during her convalescent period, she lifted her tear-stained face toward heaven, where she encountered Almighty God as a transformative power that provided healing to her battered spirit, endowing her with a passion for living life to the fullest extent possible. With every fiber of her being reverberating with resurrection possibilities, Joni Eareckson Tada became an ambassador of hope to millions of people, people who desperately need to hear the liberating message that life need not end with the onset of adversity.

We Must Embrace Difficult Times

In those instances when we are encumbered by adversity, not only is it disorienting to our sense of well-being, but it also proves to be extremely life-diminishing because it saps our vitality and strip-mines our enthusiasm for living, attempting to convince us that there is absolutely no rational reason for pressing on. Difficult experiences oftentimes subject us to states of depression, disillusionment, and despair, where it becomes a titanic struggle to visualize any meaningful life beyond the crippling pain of the moment. But while it is no easy task in struggling to maintain a positive outlook on the future when these dark states take hold, we must cultivate the will to battle the encroaching paralysis by pressing our way with God's help through the maze of emotions that come in tow with difficulties that threaten to degrade our lives.

As painful as the journey toward healing invariably proves to be, the only way of recapturing a semblance of wholeness is to forge ahead step by painful step. And the only way of initiating this life-changing activity is to begin the process. Lessons from history teach us that in those instances when we are confronted with difficult experiences, healing always exists at some point in the future. But we will never experience transformation of our life situation if we fail to embark on the journey of climbing our steep hill of recovery by moving forward in faith. In order to break adversity's stranglehold on our existence, we must give ourselves to the quickening power of the Holy Spirit so that the life of God might perform its redeeming and reparative work to aspects of our being in need of transformation.

Writing about three decades ago in her groundbreaking treatise entitled *On Death and Dying: What the Dying Have to Teach Doctors, Nurses, Clergy and Their Own Family*, the late Dr. Elizabeth Kübler-Ross, M.D., delineated the five stages of the grieving process, which her illuminating research as a clinical psychiatrist working with terminally ill patients concluded that they are compelled to grapple with—*denial, anger, bargaining, depression*, and *acceptance*.[13]

Dr. Kübler-Ross was a resident psychiatrist at Billings Hospital in Chicago, where she was involved in teaching divinity students about caring for the terminally ill. To her dismay, she discovered that there was very little data upon which a structured approach could be established. After experiencing some initial resistance from certain members of the urban institution's medical staff, Dr. Kübler-Ross eventually received permission from the institution's administration to conduct a series of interviews with very sick and dying patients. Her interviews were conducted in the confines of a special room, while the student audience, which at times numbered well into the 50s, observed the interview process through a screen window. The interviews were open-ended, and the vast majority of the patients were receptive to her investigative pursuits. The groundbreaking research enabled her to develop a five-stage process, which was later published in a book that received literary acclaim. It also became a helpful tool in assisting medical personnel and clergy gain a deeper insight about the stages of death and dying. More importantly, Dr. Kübler Ross's findings brought much-needed attention to the needs of terminally ill patients, and became a springboard for a growing movement toward compassionate care of the dying.

The first stage of the dying process posited by Dr. Kübler-Ross consists of the *denial* that ensues from the shock of the diagnosis. In those instances when individuals are confronted with episodes of sickness that bring them face-to-face with their impending mortality, the initial reaction is to deny what is happening to them. Because of the tendency to deny that something horrific might be eroding their sense of well-being, individuals who are confronted with life-threatening illnesses frequently tend to dis-associate themselves from reality. They refuse to acknowledge the existence of a malevolent force in whose clutches they find themselves hostage.

After the unsettling reality sets in, they enter the second stage of the process, where they oftentimes direct *anger* toward God, laying blame at the Creator's doorstep for either causing or allowing difficulties unimpeded reign to disrupt the tranquility of their lives. They might even question, "How could He do this to me?" Yet again, they might direct anger toward close family members, mostly because of what these individuals represent—life and health.

In a desperate attempt to escape their apparent fate, patients enter into the third stage of the cycle, which Dr. Kübler-Ross describes as *bargaining*. The bargaining stage consists of two components. The first is a secular bargain with the patient's doctor and family, and the second is a religious bargain with God. In each instance, patients offer something in exchange for reprieve from their pain-predicament. Usually it is a promise to adhere to the treatment protocols of physicians, whose expertise they expect will garner them a much-desired extended lease on life. And in the case of religious individuals, it might be a promise to regularly attend a house of worship or give to charity.

When no reprieve is forthcoming, the fourth stage sets in: *depression*. As the onset of illness takes a heavy toll on patients and their energy gradually wanes, they ultimately feel the full impact of their prognosis. Under the awful strain, the suffering souls can no longer ignore reality and eventually acknowledge the irreparable loss of a significant portion of their well-being. The fifth stage, *acceptance*, sets in, though not all dying people reach this stage.[14]

It is not uncommon for individuals who are confronted with difficulties that are potentially life-threatening, and non-life-threatening, to exhibit symptoms that mimic the five stages of the grief cycle posited by Dr. Kübler-Ross. It is important to note, however, that in certain instances individuals might not experience every stage of the cycle, but occasionally bypass one or more of them. Yet again, individuals might move back and forth between different stages of the cycle. And further still, different stages of the cycle might occur simultaneously.[15] Each episode of illness has its unique dynamic. As such, it is extremely beneficial to sufferers when they are fortunate enough to receive assistance working their way through the full range of the cycle from therapists who are skilled in the discipline of grief counseling. Since breaking free from pain's viscous grip is a feat that is difficult to accomplish alone, it is beneficial for suffering folk to solicit the expertise of skilled therapists who can provide them with strategies that can enable them to cope with the trauma impacting their life situation, thereby rendering them more adept at navigating the various stages of the cycle.

Skilled therapists are acutely aware of the fact that every episode of difficulty is not necessarily life-threatening. However, in those instances when trauma ensuing from non-life-threatening episodes is not adequately addressed, the situation could fester and become progressively worse. Peter A. Levine indicates that trauma is the most avoided, ignored, belittled, denied, misunderstood, and untreated cause of human suffering. He contends that while trauma is a source of tremendous distress and dysfunction, it is not in itself an ailment or a disease, but merely the by-product of an instinctively instigated altered state of consciousness. Levine argues that in those instances when we become overwhelmed by a perceived threat to our sense of well-being and rendered incapable of summoning the resources needed to emancipate ourselves, we are predisposed to becoming "stuck" in survival mode. This highly aroused state is designed solely to facilitate short-term defensive actions; but if left untreated over time, it begins to generate symptoms of trauma. These symptoms have the potential of insinuating themselves in every aspect of our existence and are powerful enough to distort the very fabric of our individual, cultural, economic, political, religious, and spiritual aspirations.[16]

The inability to adequately address the emotions ensuing from difficult experiences oftentimes results in suffering folk becoming "stuck" at various stages of the grief cycle, influencing them to short-circuit the full range of the cycle. Emotions are natural feelings, and they affect our ability to think critically, causing us to view our pain-predicament in an unnatural light. In this vein, we must struggle to prevent emotions from overwhelming us, because embracing negative thoughts could lead to foreclosure of a bright future, causing us to remain entrapped in our pain-predicament. Even in those instances when we are inclined to believe that we are confronted with the worst that life could throw at us, we must remain open to entrusting our circumstances to the providential care of Almighty God, thereby denying pain and suffering the opportunity to victimize and paralyze us. *We must always remember that in those instances when we turn away from God, we turn away from the sole answer to our suffering.* It is important to believe that God will provide us with insight to address our pain-predicament, thereby enabling us to move from a place of suffering to a place of redemption and renewal.

German theologian Jurgen Moltman reminds us that we serve a God with "future as his essential nature," because the Creator is forever doing a new thing.[17] Like Moltman, the psalmist points to a future reality: *"Weeping may endure for a night, but joy cometh in the morning"* (Ps. 30:5). God's light-flushed promises point to a joyous sunrise following each onset of despair. Therefore, in those instances when we are impacted by the difficulties of life, our primary objective ought to be that of courageously walking by faith through the velvet darkness of adversity so we arrive in the illuminating rays of God's transformative light. Despite the absence of visible landmarks that provide us with concrete assurances of being on the right track, the apostle Paul exhorts us to walk by faith, not by sight (see 2 Cor. 5:7), being confident that our heavenly Father will never let us down. In those instances when we are conflicted by feelings of uncertainty, it is comforting to embrace the admonition of the great American civil rights icon and Nobel Peace Prize winner, the late Reverend Dr. Martin Luther King Jr., who is credited with having said, "Take the first step in faith. You don't have to see the whole staircase. Just take the first step."

In his divinely inspired composition of the 23rd Psalm, David declared: *"Yea, though I walk through the valley of the shadow of death, I will fear no evil*" (Ps. 23:4). Armed with uncommon wisdom born of his experiences as a sojourner, who was compelled on repeated occasions to traverse the rough side of the mountain, the language employed by the sweet psalmist of Israel indicates that the journey from brokenness to wholeness entails the cultivation of spiritual defiance, because God cannot accomplish His work of transformation within us if we are intent on remaining passive and inert. While God stands ready to transform us, He will not "walk" for us. From a spiritual perspective, "walking" involves allowing God into the moments of our life situation and allowing the Holy Spirit to accomplish His work of transformation within us. God does not expect us to have things all figured out in our heads before we undertake our journey of moving toward healing. He simply expects us to move ahead in faith, relying exclusively on His power to take us to a place of restoration.

The struggle to recapture a semblance of wholesomeness in those instances when painful experiences lash us like a whip is by no means an illusory walk in the park. Instead, it subjects us to the unsettling experience of being bounced up and down in an unpredictable and disorienting roller-coaster ride. But despite the pain assaulting our spirit in those instances when we are impacted by adversity, we must forge ahead through the maze of difficulties, relying on the power of Almighty God to grant us the resources to battle hidden and mysterious forces, confident that our heavenly Father will add something to our nature from the supernatural realm, capable of taking us safely through the valley. This sentiment is echoed in a psalm attributed to the Sons of Korah: "*Blessed is the man whose strength is in Thee; in whose heart are the ways of them. Who passing though the valley of Baca make it a well; the rain also filleth the pools*" (Ps. 84:5-6).

Despite valley experiences when adversity surged through David's life with tsunami-like ferociousness, the legacy bequeathed to history by Israel's favorite son entails that of being a man after God's own heart (see 1 Sam. 13:14). Scripture credits David with being a man after God's own heart, not only because he struggled to make God the highest dimension of his existence and acknowledged sin in his life, but because he recognized the need to avail himself to succor and sustenance from the Creator that proved to be pivotal in the transformation of his life situation. The recurring sentiment embedded in the lines of numerous psalms attributed to the authorship of David indicates that in those instances when he arrived at the end of his self-sufficiency, he acknowledged God as his all-sufficiency—his true source of help. By relinquishing the keys to his kingdom of self-sufficiency to God and acknowledging the Creator as his all-sufficiency, David "lost his soul" in order that he might find it.

In addition to being a man after God's own heart, history endows David with the unique distinction of being Israel's most beloved king. However, not unlike scores of his fellow human beings, David was inflicted with proverbial feet of clay, and displayed a sinister side of his personality. He was a cold-blooded murderer and adulterer. He conspired with his ambitious and unscrupulous nephew Joab to orchestrate the death of Uriah the Hittite, one of the king's loyal generals, and someone who was numbered among the elite coterie of his 37 mighty men (see 1 Chron. 11:41). David's mastermind of the scheme that resulted in Uriah's death was an attempt to conceal the fact that he had impregnated Bathsheba, Uriah's beloved wife, while the general was away from home providing leadership to a military campaign against the Ammonite nation at their capital city of Rabbah (see 2 Sam. 11–12). After he was confronted with incriminating evidence of his sin by Nathan, the prophet of God at the royal court in Jerusalem during his reign and the early years of his son Solomon, David recognized the wisdom of discontinuing any further cover-up of his devious behavior. He acknowledged his sin before Almighty God, and beseeched the Creator: *"Create in me a clean heart, O God; and renew a right spirit within me"* (Ps. 51:10).

God's word admonishes us to keep our heart with all diligence, because from the heart spring the issues of life (see Prov. 4:23). From a physiological point of view, cardiologists recognize the heart as the organ designed by the Creator for pumping blood through the interior universe of interconnecting tubules that comprise the human circulatory system. However, in biblical language, the heart is frequently referred to as the seat of emotions and the centrality of *motivation* in the God/human relationship. It is the command center of an individual. As such, David recognized the need to acquire a heart capable of producing outcomes 180 degrees different from those that were generated by the impulses of his self. Even though he had it all—wealth, power, position, and prestige—his heart was influenced by impulses that generated outcomes that were hopelessly out of synch with the principles stipulated in God's word. He recognized that his native intelligence was incapable of engendering the transformation of his life situation. So he surrendered the nerve center of his consent to God (see Matt. 16:25).

This orientation to life enabled him to entrust his heart to God's heart by recognizing Him as sovereign, and the One capable of effectuating transformation of his life situation. *Sovereign* means that God is in control. It means that He is sufficient for all that we need. And it means that our heavenly Father has the final word on how things will turn out in our life situation. The acknowledgement of God's sovereignty over every facet of David's life situation illuminated the folly of his self-centered worldview, compelling him to engage in a self-emptying surrender that ushered him to the threshold of God's all-sufficiency. The embrace of God's all-sufficiency resulted in the transformation of David's life, and birthed a spirit of humility within the bosom of the youngest son of Jesse. Simone Weil states, "Humility is the refusal to exist outside of God. It is the queen of virtues."[18]

The posture of humility adopted by David when he aligned his will with the will of the Almighty liberated him from his illusions about being the captain of his destiny and provided him with a heart that generated positive outcomes in his life situation. C.S. Lewis contends that humility is a kind of death whereby we surrender our self-sufficiency to God, thereby affording Him the opportunity to put a little bit of Himself into us. Lewis argues that God avails us a little bit of His reasoning powers, teaching us to think in a new way, and shares His nature with us.[19] The new heart provided to David by the Creator, convinced him of the need to die to self-sufficiency in order that he might experience God's all-sufficiency. The embrace of God's all-sufficiency served to transfigure David's spiritual DNA, enabling his heart to beat in tandem with the divine rhythm, garnering him outcomes that were opposite those that were generated by the impulses of his misguided heart.

David's life experiences illuminate the fact that liberation from difficulties has a syntax all its very own. They lend credence to the fact that the journey to liberation is a migratory path with its genesis in humility, coursing through numerous way stations in an upward climb that culminates in a transformed reality—God's new thing. As such, humility is the first rung on the ladder of recovery we are exhorted to grab hold of as we co-labor with God in unshackling ourselves from the life-diminishing forces, that we might embark on the life-enlarging pilgrimage of transformation.

Reflection Questions

Several questions are presented at the end of each chapter that might be utilized for personal meditation, spiritual direction sessions, or small group discussions.

1. Does the occurrence of painful events influence you to question the sovereignty of God over the universe?

2. Do you view the difficulties impacting your life as unmerited suffering?

3. Using Scripture as a guide, what advice would you offer to individuals whose lives are being impacted by difficult circumstances?

CHAPTER TWO

Remain Humble During Difficult Times

At some point on our earthly pilgrimage, we are inevitably awakened to one of life's oft-ignored realities, namely, that there are some bridges we will be unable to cross under our own power. In our journey up life's road, we will be confronted by circumstances so unsettling that we will experience difficulty untangling ourselves from our predicament and will require divine help in order to experience liberation. As David arrived at the end of his self-sufficiency, giving God the opportunity to convince him of his need for divine help, in like manner God will in some way engineer circumstances that bring us to the end of our self-sufficiency so that He might convince us of our need for divine help.

After being compelled to flee the environs of Jerusalem in order to evade further attempts on his life by his father-in-law Saul, who repeatedly sought to kill him with a javelin, David roamed the countryside as a fugitive outlaw, accompanied by his immediate family and a 400-man army that followed him into exile. With the passage of time, the number of individuals accompanying David surged to approximately 600 men.

During David's tenure in exile, Israel's army suffered a crushing defeat at the hands of their Philistine neighbors on the slopes of Mount Gilboa, in the Jezreel Valley. During the battle, Saul and his three sons, Abinadab, Malchishua, and Jonathan, his favorite and apparent heir, were all killed. The death of Saul and the three princes represented a watershed event in the history of the Hebrew nation, leaving it without a designated heir. In accordance with the ancient custom of primogeniture, the eldest surviving son of a king usually ascended the throne to assume leadership on the event of his father's death. However, since there was no surviving heir to the throne on the event of Saul's demise and that of the three princes, the elders of Israel sought David out in the city of Hebron, where he had established his headquarters after being run out of town by Saul. After much persuasion, the elders convinced the youthful 30-year-old battle-tested warrior to assume the mantle of king and commander-in-chief over the 12 tribes of the confederacy.

David's tenure as king was a high point in the nation's history. Not only did Israel experience spectacular military victories over external enemies that resulted in the expansion of the nation's territorial borders, it also cemented alliances with several neighbors that served its national interests. In lieu of his rich experiences with God, one might have expected that David would have developed the sturdiest possible confidence in the Creator that prevented him from engaging in aspects of behavior that were displeasing to God. Unfortunately, such was not the case. At an advanced age, he committed a sin that produced disastrous outcomes. While his own life was spared, David's actions resulted in God's wrath being unleashed against Israel, resulting in the death of innocent civilians. Scripture tells us: *"And Satan stood up against Israel, and provoked David to number Israel"* (1 Chron. 21:1).

While the Old Testament narrative does not provide any concrete reasons as to why David felt compelled to number Israel, any speculation on his motives is pure conjecture. There are, however, those who subscribe to the belief that during this narrow neck of history, the aged king might very well have entertained the belief that the troops on active duty in his army were not up to the task of safeguarding Israel against potential enemy incursions. If we follow this line of argument, this mindset might very well have influenced David to believe that he needed reinforcements to bolster the ranks of his army. Tormented by feelings of insecurity that gnawed at his spirit, David instructed his field commanders to conduct a national census that would provide him with information concerning the number of able-bodied men in the general population, 20 years and older, who could be mobilized to active duty in the event of a military conflict with a potential enemy.

Under the Law of Moses, census taking was not inherently evil, as evidenced by the Old Testament report where God on two separate occasions commanded the prophet Moses to number the Israelite nation—once in the second year after they were emancipated from Egyptian bondage, and again about 40 years later, toward the end of Israel's wandering in the desert (see Num. 1:1-3,19; 26:2-4). However, a person's motives can at times turn lawful actions into sinful deeds (see Matt. 6:1-8). Such might have been the case when David took it upon himself to number the Israelites at some point during the sunset of his reign. It is quite clear that at no point does Scripture indicate that God instructed David to conduct the census, nor does it indicate that he instigated the census taking for some noble purpose. But his actions lead us to believe that he was relying on human strength to attain some unknown outcome instead of relying on the all-sufficiency of Almighty God.

Suspicious of the king's motives for numbering Israel, David's nephew and the commander of Israel's army, Joab, cautioned him to refrain from pursuing the unwise course of action. David remained obstinate, insisting that he be provided with the vital statistics from which he could glean information pertaining to the number of potential recruits that could be mobilized to active duty in the event of war. But after being provided with the information that he requested from his subordinates, he became convicted concerning his foolish actions, and recognized the need to engage in a process of self-correction. David's introspection prompted him to reset his inner ethical clock in order to correct the error of fallen priorities and assumptions about power and security. It enabled him to recognize that Israel's successes on the battlefield ensued exclusively from the providence of Almighty God, and not from the might of the nation's powerful army. As such, he recognized the need to divest himself of his illusion of self-sufficiency.

While Scripture in silent on the actual details of David's spiritual turbulence, the outcome is clear. God convinced the misguided king that He was singularly responsible for orchestrating his ascendancy to the throne of Israel by pointing out that He instructed the prophet Samuel to anoint David as successor to his disobedient and insecure predecessor Saul at a feast in Bethlehem in the presence of his entire family (see 1 Sam. 16:13). God, in ways that only He can, drove home to David the reality that his spectacular victories on the battlefield were at no time contingent on political calculations or military prowess, but ensued exclusively from divine providence. God revealed to David that He was all the security he needed.

Humility: Acknowledging God As Sovereign Over Our Lives

After acknowledging that he had committed a colossal blunder, David recognized the need to make atonement for his sin. God responded to the aged king's contrition by presenting him with three options of punishment from which to choose. The first option entailed having seven years of famine ravage the nation of Israel. The second option required that he vacate the precincts of Jerusalem for three months while being pursued by enemies. And the third option involved having three days of pestilence leveled against the land.

Responding to the options presented to him by the prophet Gad, the emissary saddled with the grim task of conveying God's ill tidings to the conflicted king, David lamented: *"I am in great distress; let us fall into the hand of the Lord, for His mercy is great; but let me not fall into human hands"* (2 Sam. 24:14 NRSV). Despite David's contrition, God unleashed a punishing plague against Israel that wreaked havoc in the tribal area of Dan in the north, and marched across the land like an alien invader into the precincts of Beersheba in the south, snuffing out 70,000 souls in its deadly wake.

David agonized over the fact that innocent lives were lost as a direct result of his reckless behavior, prompting him to embrace a spirit of humility, and acknowledging the all-sufficiency of God over the minutest facet of his life situation. His acknowledgement is reflected in the declaration: *"O Lord, God of our ancestors, are You not God in heaven? Do You not rule over all the kingdoms of the nations?"* (2 Chron. 20:6 NRSV).

He again demonstrated his acknowledgement of God's sovereignty over his life circumstances on the occasion of Solomon's ascendancy to the throne of Israel, when he admonished the newly anointed king:

> *And you, my son Solomon, know the God of your father,*
> *and serve Him with single mind and willing heart; for the*
> *Lord searches every mind, and understands every plan*
> *and thought. If you seek Him, He will be found by you;*
> *but if you forsake Him, He will abandon you forever. Take*
> *heed now, for the Lord has chosen you to build a house as*
> *the sanctuary; be strong, and act* (1 Chronicles 28:9-10
> NRSV).

Just as David acknowledged God's sovereignty over his life situation, so too Jesus departed the Trinity and became clothed in human flesh as a male Galilean Jew, to serve, die, and redeem the world back to His heavenly Father. And in order to accomplish this feat, He acknowledged His heavenly Father's sovereignty over His life situation by *humbling* Himself, and becoming an obedient servant (see Phil. 2:7-8). Jesus was the humility of God garbed in the flesh of humanity.

Paralleling the Old Testament report of David's awakening to God's all-sufficiency is another enduring testimonial of humility recorded in the synoptic Gospels—the story of the woman with the so-called "issue of blood" (see Matt. 9:20-22; Mark 5:20-29; Luke 6:6-11). While the definitive nature of the woman's illness is anybody's guess, there is a prevailing consensus among medical authorities and biblical scholars, subscribing to the possibility that she was afflicted with an irregularity of her female reproductive system. While the source of bleeding is not specified in any of the biblical texts, commentators on Scripture hold to the likelihood of vaginal or uterine bleeding. The Septuagint (the Greek translation of the Hebrew Scriptures) employs the identical phrase in Leviticus referring to bleeding that is presumably vaginal (see Lev. 15:19,25; 20:18), shedding some illumination on the widely held assumption.

Even though there is no conclusive evidence as to what the woman's definitive medical problem might have been, if we assume that her problem was vaginal bleeding, we should note that she was afflicted with an abnormal condition. Her malady did not appear to be menstruation, which is a normal, healthy female condition, but was in all likelihood a menstrual disorder of some sort. Whatever the presenting diagnosis might have been, Scripture indicates that she was sick and compelled to consult with several physicians, who oftentimes treated her shabbily. When the physicians realized that they were on unchartered clinical terrain and lacked the ability to cure the patient of the besetting malady, they unceremoniously discharged her from treatment, sending her home to die.

Instead of surrendering to the disease and giving up, the suffering soul continued seeking a source of healing for the plague that laid siege to her body for 12 pain-wracked years. Her persistence eventually paid off when she received exhilarating news that a miracle-working rabbi from Nazareth would soon be paying a visit to her community. After being appraised of the route by which the itinerant preacher would be entering the community, she positioned herself at a location that would afford her ample opportunity to be in close proximity with this person from Nazareth when He passed by. She thought to herself, *"If I but touch His clothes, I will be made well"* (Mark 5:28 NRSV).

As Jesus approached the place where the woman waited with eager anticipation to establish contact with Him, she refused to be denied healing and intruded on the scene, injecting her fragile frame into the sea of humanity, intentionally grabbing hold of one of the tassels of His rabbinical garment. The moment she touched the fringes of His prayer shawl, referred to in the New Testament as the "hem" of His garment (see Num. 15:37-41; Matt. 9:20), the flow of blood dried up, and she recognized in her body that her plague was over and done with. The stream of divine energy emanating from the person of Jesus surged like a healing current through the woman's wraith-like body, reversing the decay and providing her with a semblance of wholeness.

When Jesus discerned that energy had been discharged from His body, He turned His attention to the crowd and questioned, *"Who touched My clothes?"* (Mark 5:30 NRSV). The disciples were puzzled over the unexpected inquiry, and pointed out to the Master that they were immersed in an animated crowd that kept jostling each other, every person struggling against all odds to secure an audience with Him. As such, it was certainly a strange question of wanting to know who touched Him.

Well aware of the fact that in this particular instance He had been subjected to no casual touch, Jesus ignored the comments of the clueless disciples and continued peering into the vast gallery of faces, repeating what His befuddled disciples considered to be a strange question. Recognizing the change that recently transpired in her body to be the direct result of the impartation she received from the person of Jesus when she grabbed hold of the hem of His garment, and knowing that she was the recipient of divine healing, the woman stepped forward from the tide of humanity, knelt before the Master in a display of humility, and tearfully relayed the unfolding of her life story to Him. After listening to the amazing report of the woman's emancipation from the throes of torment,

Jesus provided her with the comforting words: *"Daughter, your faith has made you well; go in peace, and be healed of your disease"* (Mark 5:34 NRSV).

Humility: Recognizing the Need to Surrender Difficult Circumstances to God

In a similar manner as David surrendered his pain-predicament to God, the woman with the issue of blood also arrived at the end of her rope when she surrendered her circumstances to Almighty God. And like David, she acknowledged the sovereignty of the Creator over every facet of her life situation, and availed herself to impartation of His healing power in order to become a recipient of *shalom*—His all-around goodness and harmony for her life, where nothing is broken or nothing is missing. She arrived at the realization that healing becomes a reality in the lives of God's children when they entrust their circumstances to the Healer from Galilee. Armed with this life-changing illumination, she sought an encounter with the Healer from Galilee.

Scripture indicates that after consulting with several medical practitioners within her local community, the suffering soul experienced absolutely no respite from her malady. Being human, the inability of the physicians to provide her with much-needed respite from her pain-predicament undoubtedly subjected her to feelings of disappointment and depression. Not only did the physicians discover that they were unable to provide her with a viable cure for the malady that eroded her sense of well-being, but due to ineffective treatment protocols that were employed to address her persistent medical condition, her sickness became progressively worse with each passing day, spiraling down, rendering her more distraught and helpless. Unable to stanch the escalation of her deteriorating medical condition, the clinical masters discharged her as an incurable patient. While they undoubtedly had noble intentions of some day ascertaining the root cause of the patient's pathology, they merely compounded her pain-predicament before acknowledging that they were at their wits' end, and recognized the wisdom of curtailing further medical intervention.

There are instances in life when we attempt to fix problems that ultimately only God can fix. And repeated attempts to bring about problem resolution only serve to make matters worse. Inflicted with hubris as pride, which is referred to in the Greek language, we at times refuse to acknowledge that we will encounter problems whose resolution is speaking "over our heads." As such, we tend to complicate matters when we neglect to petition God for the impartation of insight so we can receive illumination concerning besetting problems. In the long run, we run up against a brick wall and recognize that the only thing we accomplish in those instances when we refuse to seek God's assistance is the compounding of existing problems, thereby making matters worse off than they were before.

Like the dumbfounded physicians who were unable to unlock the puzzle of the woman's dilemma, we eventually recognize the wisdom of abandoning our posture of self-sufficiency by turning our problem situation over to the agency of Almighty God. Abandoning our posture of self-sufficiency entails entrusting our limitations to the all-knowing power of our heavenly Father in order that He might provide us with a perspective from the dimension of the eternal. Abandoning our posture of self-sufficiency additionally brings us to the place where we recognize the wisdom of looking for help to that which is stronger than ourselves.

We must always bear in mind that when we speak of entrusting problems to God, it does not mean that we merely dump them in the Creator's lap, casually walking away with the expectation that He will resolve them without our input or involvement. It additionally does not mean that we should abandon our agency and responsibility. It does mean, however, that we ought to work toward problem resolution in the divine presence and with divine assistance. Scripture informs us: *"What is impossible for mortals is possible for God"* (Luke 18:27 NRSV). When we recognize the wisdom of turning to God for help, He will reward our confidence in His ability by providing impartation to us, and do for us that which we are unable to do for ourselves with our limited insight (see Matt. 7:7). Attempting to resolve intractable problems with a limited scope of options invariably proves to be ineffective in bringing about problem resolution, as evidenced by the efforts of the physicians in their attempts to provide healing to the sick woman. However, in those instances when we seek impartation from God, our heavenly Father will provide us with an array of options that could be employed in the successful resolution of life's besetting problems.

Humility: Turning Toward God

In the process of surrendering her pain predicament to God, the woman with the issue of blood engaged in two distinct activities. The first activity entailed changing the direction from which she previously looked to for help, even though she might have been compelled to do so against her will when the physicians discharged her from treatment as a hopeless case.

Turning to God involves changing our spiritual orientation in those instances when we are spinning our wheels and going nowhere fast, because attempting to bring about the transformation of negative life situations without turning away from the forces that generate or perpetuate those situations is utterly futile. *Continuing to rely on forces that generate or perpetuate negative life situations merely compound our pain-predicament, because relying on such forces relegates us to states of stagnation and prevents us from arriving at the threshold of healing.* Therefore, in order to experience transformation of our life situation, we must disengage ourselves from forces that generate or perpetuate negative life situations and turn toward the source that is able to provide us with a new reality—Almighty God.

The Bible tells us that we are God's creation. This means that our existence is rooted in the *imago Dei*. It additionally means that God is intimately acquainted with every facet of our human makeup, and knows what makes His creatures tick. David sheds illumination on this truth by reminding us that we are fearfully and wonderfully made (see Ps. 139:14). As such, when we turn away from life-negating forces and turn to the Creator by acknowledging His sovereignty over our life, He will provide us with impartation that enables us to resolve problems whose resolution resides beyond the scope of our limited insight. God is the source from which all reasoning power comes.

Far too many people go through life unable to experience transformation in their life situation because they rely on the wrong sources for problem resolution instead of relying on God. Failing to recognize the futility of their actions, they live with the illusion that they will someday attain resolution of their problem situation. The Bible tells us that when we turn to God for help, the Holy Spirit "endues us with power from on high" (see Acts 1:8; Luke 24:49). God is all-powerful and will avail us power that enlivens the circuits of our spirit, transforming and transfiguring every aspect of our life situation as we enter into deeper dimensions with Him and partake of His divine nature.

Transformation involves moving up to a higher plane of existence from a former place in which we were burdened by limitations of every sort. It entails the old giving way to the new, because transformation by the Holy Spirit changes us from that which we once were into new creatures. Transformation becomes a reality in the lives of God's children when we submit every aspect of our life situation to the governance of Almighty God. Employing the language of the apostle Paul: *"Everything old has passed away; see, everything has become new!"* (2 Cor. 5:17 NRSV). In order for us to become the recipients of supernatural power from Almighty God, we must refrain from seeking transformation in life-negating sources, turn in the direction of God, and open our spirit to the impartation that He offers us. God cannot change us if we are not receptive to that which He desires us to have. In the words of Augustine, "God gives where he finds empty hands."[1]

Humility: Positioning Ourselves to Experience Holy Encounters With God

The second activity that the woman with the issue of blood engaged in involved that of positioning herself at a location where she could experience a life-changing encounter with the person of Jesus. The woman recognized Jesus as God incarnate, and the assumption of her position reflected the radicalization of her consciousness. Instead of relying exclusively on the clinical expertise of the medical practitioners to provide her with a semblance of healing as she previously did, she now recognized the wisdom of entrusting her circumstances to the Healer from Galilee. As such, establishing contact with Jesus became the ultimate encounter— the turning point of her situation.

The spiritual posture or orientation that we assume in life is a direct reflection of our desire to experience a divine encounter with God so that we might receive impartation from Him. The Psalmist declared: *"I lift up my eyes to the hills—from where will my help come? My help comes from the Lord, who made heaven and earth"* (Ps. 121:1-2 NRSV). *Hills* in biblical parlance allude to states of higher consciousness. In his composition of the beautiful psalm, the poet revealed that his mind was stretched toward Almighty God so he might experience impartation that would enable him to transcend his limitations. His orientation to life reflected the ardent desire of experiencing union with God, that he might become the recipient of succor and sustenance from the source of life. The psalmist's sentiment is congruent with the utterance of the apostle Paul on the occasion of his Aeropagus Sermon, when he declared: *"For 'In Him we live and move and have our being'; as even some of your own poets have said"* (Acts 17:28 NRSV). Paul's language identifies God as the source and sustainer of all life. It highlighted that, when we avail ourselves to impartation from the Almighty, we become conduits of His divine nature. By sharing His own self and almighty power with His creation, God empowers us to endure adversity of the worst kind.

While it is possible to encounter God at any place and time, we might choose to encounter Him by placing ourselves at designated locations. For example, pilgrimages to "sacred spaces" reflect a burning desire to experience meaningful encounters with the Creator. They denote the expectation of encountering God in our sanctuary or "tent of meeting." It might prove to be spiritually refreshing to occasionally journey to venues of intimacy or sacred places in order to escape the hustle and bustle of noisy surroundings. Even though they do not actually possess any inherent sacredness in and of themselves, they become sacred when we recognize the fact that God is everywhere. Wherever God inhabits becomes sacred, because God's habitation is a place of unlimited possibilities. Additionally, sacred places afford us an atmosphere of tranquility that enables us to create space in our hearts for God.

Jesus, on repeated occasions, abandoned the trappings of disquietude within the environs of the noisy city limits, and slipped away into the solitude of the Judean hills, where He spent extensive hours in communion with His heavenly Father. Our Lord's sojourns into the wilderness were attempts to find clarity about His relationship with His heavenly Father and His call to ministry. His times of solitude serve as sterling examples as to how we ought to conduct ourselves during our struggle to cultivate the closest possible walk with God. Scripture informs us that God rewards those who seek Him (see Heb. 11:6). And in those instances when we undertake pilgrimages to arenas of quietude to better commune with our heavenly Father, it signifies that we are serious about experiencing an encounter with the Lover of our soul. God always honors the efforts of His children to experience meaningful encounters with Him, and will give us divine impartation to those who embark on pilgrimages of enduring the extra mile to do so. When we ask our heavenly Father for bread, He never responds by giving us a stone (see Matt. 7:9). Thomas Merton reminds us, "God gives Himself to those who give themselves to Him."[2]

C.S. Lewis concurs with the sentiments of Merton, indicating that when it comes to knowing God, the initiative lies on the Creator's side. He argues that if God does not show Himself, nothing we do will enable us to find Him. Lewis indicates that God shows much more of Himself to some people than to others—not because He has favorites, but because it is impossible for the Creator to reveal Himself to individuals whose mind and character are oriented in the wrong condition, just as sunlight, though it has no favorites, cannot be reflected in a dusty mirror as clearly as a clean one. Lewis further indicates that in sciences beside theology, the instruments utilized are things external to one's self (things like microscopes and telescopes). However, in theology, the instrument through which we see God is the whole self. And if a man or woman's self is not kept clean and bright, his or her glimpse of God will be blurred—like the moon seen through a dirty telescope.[3] *The whole long and short of the matter is that God reveals Himself to those who avail themselves to Him so they might experience meaningful encounters with divine love that culminate in a deepened life of faith.* Augustine purportedly stated someplace, "The God who created us without our consent, will not save us without our consent," which corroborates this truth.

As it pertains to receiving impartation from God, Merton informs us that our seeking God does not consist of us finding Him by means of certain ascetic techniques. He indicates that it is through the quieting and ordering of our whole life by self-denial, prayer, and good works, that God Himself, who seeks us more that we seek Him, might "find us" and "take possession of us."[4]

Humility: Taking Risks

When Jesus discerned that energy had been discharged from His body and questioned His disciples as to who touched His person, the woman who was cured of the issue of blood had every reason to hesitate acknowledging that she was the one who touched Him. She was the resident of an ancient society in which women were denied full equality with their male counterparts. And in lieu of the inequality circumscribing her daily existence, she was relegated to the status of second-class citizenry that severely limited her access to rabbis. Additionally, Jewish religious law prohibited physical contact between unmarried couples of the opposite sex. Even though she was intimately aware of the stringent religious taboo that prohibited her from touching a male, she summoned the requisite courage and forcefully propelled her fragile frame through the bustling throng of humanity that surrounded Jesus, purposely grabbing hold of the hem of His garment. While this was audacious in and of itself, she further placed herself in a precarious position on account of her intractable medical condition.

Jewish religious laws of ancient Israel relegated the woman to the status of being "unclean" on account of her incessant hemorrhaging, thereby signifying that she was someone to be avoided for the duration of her menstrual cycle (see Lev. 15:19). Additionally, her continuous bleeding (if vaginal) placed her in a state of perpetual cultic impurity, as outlined in the law (see Lev. 15:25). On account of her intractable medical condition, anyone who touched her would summarily be rendered "unclean," which further complicated her life. As such, any rabbi who had knowledge of her medical condition would go to extra lengths to avoid establishing contact with her to prevent him from being burdened with the annoying requirement of having to submit to a mandatory period of ritual cleansing before being able to resume his religious duties (see Lev. 15:19).

Even though she was intimately aware of the prohibitions circumscribing her daily existence, the woman disregarded the ancient religious taboo, courageously ventured beyond the boundaries of established protocol, and took action to do something about her situation so she could receive healing from God. The courageous act indicated that she wanted more from God, and that nothing was more important to her than that of securing an encounter with the Healer from Nazareth, even if it necessitated taking enormous risks and swimming against the tide of the prevailing religious tradition.

By violating the time-honored codes of the ancient rabbinical tradition and repeatedly healing sick people on the hallowed Jewish Sabbath, Jesus took risks in His efforts to liberate folk that were encumbered by suffering and disease. He was ecclesiastically out of touch with the religious establishment of His day, and His disdain for the life-limiting religious conventions brought Him difficulties with His dogmatic colleagues in the rabbinical establishment (see Luke 4:32; John 9:13). Many individuals in the local community not only considered Him to be a heretic, but also a raving lunatic and someone who was out of touch with reality. Additionally, many individuals considered His words on the occasion of the grain field incident to be the height of blasphemy when He proclaimed Himself to be the self-anointed Lord of the Sabbath (see Matt. 12:8), which is the most sacred aspect of the God-given Jewish law.

However, being someone who was intent on abandoning the orthodox inflexibility of the ancient rabbinical tradition in order to dispense healing to suffering humanity, Jesus demonstrated that providing *shalom* to His heavenly Father's children was far more important than rigid adherence to the established religious protocol of His day. Our Lord's perspective on life demonstrated that nothing on earth, however sacred, should become a barrier to the liberation of His heavenly Father's suffering sons and daughters. He rewarded the woman's exercise of faith by granting her the desire of her heart, thereby demonstrating that His response to her predicament was congruent with His message to humanity: *"I came that they may have life, and have it abundantly"* (John 10:10 NRSV).

Despite repeated encounters with adversity, we must never abandon our struggle to experience a new reality or shirk from undertaking risks that will render us the recipients of transformation, because nothing great in life is ever accomplished without taking some sort of risk. God is on the side of those who are courageous enough to launch out into the deep waters of life's unlimited possibilities and engage in risk-taking in order to experience transformation of their life situation. He is intimately acquainted with the minutest aspect of our existence, and He will grant us the desires of our heart in those instances when we are determined to risk it all by throwing caution to the wind and entrusting our hope for the acquisition of abundant life exclusively on His providential care.

Jurgen Moltman indicates that hope is the key to understanding history, for the hope that flows from the promise of God creates history. The insightful theologian argues that hope is the "inseparable companion" of faith, and begs the question, "What would become of us if we did not take our stand on hope, and if our heart did not hasten beyond this world through the midst of the darkness upon the path illuminated by the word and Spirit of God!"[5]

The ancient prophet Zechariah tells us that we are prisoners of hope (see Zech. 9:12). Hope is the catalyst that fuels our quest for liberation from the confining corridors of human life. The amazing possibilities ensuing from the hope-filled life highlights the truth that God will never leave us nor forsake us, and He is eternally predisposed to granting us the desire of our hearts. Hope is numbered among the three theological virtues (see 1 Cor. 13:11), and is the next rung of the ladder we are exhorted to grab hold of as we journey from the throes of torment to a realm of redemption and reclamation.

Reflection Questions

1. How would you define *humility* in one sentence?

2. In your estimation, which biblical personalities would you consider to be models or exemplars of humility? Why?

3. Using scriptural evidence as a guide, do you believe God desires that you should strive to attain a higher level of humility?

CHAPTER THREE

Keep Hope Alive
in Difficult Times

Hope is a transcendent force that affords us a portal into the future, enabling us to visualize new possibilities—God's "new thing"—even in difficult circumstances when our fragile world threatens to split open and fall apart. It draws our gaze away from the tranquilizing status quo, pointing us to "what is possible," providing us with a horizon that is always beckoning and drawing our eyes forward.

Vincent Harding, civil rights icon and speech writer for the late Reverend Dr. Martin Luther King Jr., commented on the hope-filled life of his colleague, Howard Thurman, an African-American scholar, theologian, spiritual adviser to Dr. King, and someone hailed by *Life* magazine as one of the outstanding preachers of the 20th century: "No external force however great and overwhelming can at long last destroy a people if it does not first win the victory of the spirit against them."[1] Thurman's outlook on life supports the premise that in perilous times when we are assailed by the destructive power of dominating forces, we are still capable of attaining new horizons as long as we exercise hope for a new reality. He opines that the dawning of new experiences is eternally possible when we refuse to indulge in a complacent acceptance of the status quo and keep the embers of hope flickering within our spirit, because life's battles are ultimately won or lost in the arena of the spirit.

In those instances, when we become entrapped in a downward spiral of personal tragedy and sorrow, the ability to see clearly beyond the hurt enveloping our lives proves to be extremely difficult. We oftentimes find ourselves engaged in an ongoing struggle of managing powerful emotions while compelled to simultaneously grapple with problems so overwhelming that they threaten to rupture the fabric of our soul. Keeping a positive perspective on life is key to our survival because it enables us to summon the requisite hope, signifying that our existence need not be defined by the difficulties confronting us, but in light of who God is and what the Almighty is able to accomplish for His children. Hope is a radical act of imagination that enables us to envision transcendent possibilities that are available through faith in God. Armed with this liberating insight, scores of suffering people who were besieged with seasons of adversity survived to tell how they employed hope as a footpath to navigate their way through difficult experiences to arrive at a new station in life.

Viktor Frankl, Swiss psychiatrist, Harvard professor, and practitioner of hope, described in vivid detail in his best-selling book *Man's Search for Meaning*, how as a young prisoner in the Nazi death camps of Hitler's Third Reich, he was able to summon the necessary hope that enabled him to survive a living nightmare which scores of his fellow prisoners unfortunately did not. Frankl indicated that any prisoner who lost faith in the future, "his future" was doomed. And with the loss of belief in the future, the prisoner additionally lost his spiritual hold, allowing himself to decline and become subjected to mental and spiritual decay. The death camp survivor indicated that this state of mind usually happened suddenly, in the form of a crisis which was familiar to the experienced camp inmate. In other words, even though the inmate was intimately aware of his circumstances, he succumbed to the pressure of the ordeal and gave up on surviving when he lost hope for the future.[2]

Frankl opines that even though our present reality is shaped by events of the past, the thing that enables us to re-create the present is our vision and hope for the future. Reflecting on his death camp experience, he reports seeing inmates struggle to survive, some of whom were driven deep into despair. He additionally revealed that one of his close associates succumbed to the pressure of his ordeal and died of bitter disappointment, a mere few days before the camp in which they were incarcerated was liberated by Allied forces.

Fortunately, there were other inmates who were buoyed by their deep belief and hope in something beyond the present moment. Unlike the inmates who lost hope, these individuals experienced an inner transformation that ensued from their vision for a new reality because they exercised hope for the future. The death camp survivor wrote:

> Whoever was still alive had reason to hope. Health, family, happiness, professional abilities, fortune, position in society—all these were things that could be achieved again or restored.… I asked the poor creatures who listened to me attentively in the darkness of the hut to

face up to the seriousness of our position. They must not lose hope but should keep courage in the certainty that the hopelessness of our struggle did not detract from its dignity and its meaning.[3]

Frankl concluded that while the meaning of life always changes, it never ceases to be.[4]

Hope: Cultivating the Capacity to See "What Else," Not "What Is"

Scripture informs us that in situations described by the 4th-century Spanish mystic, John of the Cross, as the *askesis*—"the dark night of the soul"[5]—we could draw on a life much bigger than our puny lives to obtain succor and sustenance for the living of our days. This life has the power to transform our circumstances and provide us with a reality that is radically different from the difficulties in which we might be immersed at any given point in time. This truth is highlighted in the Old Testament story surrounding an occurrence in the life of the ancient prophet Elisha.

The biblical record indicates that after becoming aware of the fact that his carefully orchestrated plans to ambush the army of Israel repeatedly proved unsuccessful, the king of Syria suspected a possible breach of intelligence within the ranks of his inner circle, based on the fact that things were not turning out as planned in the theater of operations. In the attempt to identify the person responsible for "leaking" confidential information to his adversary, the king of Israel, the Syrian king convened an emergency session of his cabinet, at whose forum he relayed his suspicions to the officials in attendance. One of the officials responded to the king's concerns, informing him that there was no traitor within the Syrian camp. He then proceeded to identify the culprit as the Jewish prophet Elisha, who not only kept revealing the Syrian king's secrets to the king of Israel, but also indicated that Elisha was endowed with spiritual powers that enabled him to become privy to discussions the Syrian king conducted in the confines of his bedroom.

After identifying Elisha as the person responsible for the repeated failures of Syrian forces to ambush the army of Israel, the king of Syria deployed his troops to the city of Dothan, where Elisha was reportedly residing at the time. After arriving at Dothan, and while the city was still clothed in a cocoon of darkness, Syrian forces surrounded the military objective with the expressed purpose of apprehending the elusive Elisha. Early the following morning, Elisha's servant Gehazi ventured out into the silver glow of the emerging sunlight and peered across the landscape into the distant horizon. He was horrified when he observed countless Syrian forces strategically deployed in the rugged hills surrounding their location. Terrified at the prospects of his impending demise, he lamented to Elisha: *"Alas, master! What shall we do?"* (2 Kings 6:15 NRSV).

Elisha calmly and confidently responded to his disciple's angst-ridden query, exhorting him, *"Do not be afraid, for there are more with us than there are with them"* (2 Kings 6:16 NRSV). After assuaging the anxieties of his distraught servant, Elisha lifted a petition toward heaven, imploring: *"O Lord, please open his eyes that he may see"* (2 Kings 6:17 NRSV). In response to His prophet's petition, God endowed Gehazi with "spiritual optics" that enabled him to see "what else," instead of "what is." When he looked into the hills a second time, he observed horses and chariots of fire of the hosts of heaven encircling the Syrian army.

Because we frequently become overly preoccupied with the things we observe with our natural eyes and touch with our natural hands, we are prone to rush to the hasty conclusion that what we see and touch is the sum total of reality. Scripture informs us, however, that God is the creator *ex nihilo*—He is the agent of creation out of nothing, or He who calls into existence things that do not exist (see Rom. 4:17). We are reminded on another occasion that the things that are seen are transient, but the things that are unseen are eternal (see 2 Cor. 4:18).

On occasion, our heavenly Father deems it necessary to pull back the curtain of life, dragging our gaze away from being fixated on the current state of things in order that He might provide us with an alternate reality from that which we experience with our natural senses. This disclosure arouses within us a "passion for the possible" that is congruent with the Christian hope—hope that is directed toward a new creation of all things by the God of the resurrection of Jesus Christ. A modern-day practitioner of hope who is intimately familiar with God's power to birth new realities out of the most hellish situation is Nelson Mandela, the first democratically elected president of the nation of South Africa.

Nelson Rolihlahla Mandela was born at Mvezo, a tiny village on the banks of the Mbashe River in the district of Umtata, capital of Transkei, South Africa. He was born into the Madiba Clan of the Thembu tribe of the Xhosa Nation. His father, Nkosi Mphakanyiswa Gadla Henry, was a chief both by blood and by custom. Mandela studied law at the University of Witwatersrand in the capital city of Johannesburg, but later found himself incarcerated under maximum-security conditions in the South African prison system. He was convicted for the crime of treason after abandoning his lucrative law practice to assume top leadership of the African National Congress in its struggle to dismantle the oppressive structure of apartheid, South Africa's racial caste system that relegated blacks, Indians, and mixed races to the status of second-class citizenry.

The architects of the apartheid regime initially considered Mandela a colossal failure when his efforts to inaugurate crucial reforms in his native land appeared dashed. His life's mission to usher in an era of equality for all of South Africa's citizens by bridging the gaping chasm between the "haves" and the "have-nots" was not immediately realized, thereby prolonging the arbitrary bloodshed of innocent black, Indian, mixed-race South Africans, and progressive whites, who dared to voice their opposition against the life-withering policies of the heartless regime.

Mandela's conviction for the crime of treason consigned him to 27 long years of hard labor in South Africa's criminal justice system. Not only was he subjected to back-breaking physical labor while consigned to prison, he was also compelled to work under inhumane conditions beneath the intensity of a blazing sun in lime quarries on Robben Island, an oppressive penal colony located a distance of a little less than five miles off the coast of South Africa, in Table Bay. During its heyday as a penal facility, Robben Island was recognized as South Africa's version of America's notorious and currently shuttered Alcatraz Prison, located one and a half miles off the California coast in San Francisco Bay. Robben Island was home of the nation's unwanted: lepers, individuals that were mentally sick, political prisoners, and criminals. At one point during his lengthy incarceration, Mandela contracted the dreadful disease of pulmonary tuberculosis, and for a brief period of time his family, friends, and supporters held their collective breath because his life became threatened. Despite being compelled to endure sickness and hardships that wracked his being during the difficult years while he was consigned to prison, he remained hopeful about the dawning of a new era in his native land, and laid claim to the vision of a transformed future different from the one to which he was subjected to. Buoyed by hope for a new reality in his native land, Mandela refused to surrender to the status quo and latched on to the promises that He who is the creator *ex nihilo* and raiser of the dead would make possible.

During Mandela's incarceration in the squalid confines of the penal machinery, the gatekeepers of the apartheid regime instituted legal mandates that were specifically crafted to erase his memory from the public consciousness, deeming it an illegal act for anyone to possess a photograph or reasonable likeness of his person. Not only was the legal maneuver a systematic attempt to expunge his memory from the public consciousness, it was also an attempt to squash social reforms and maintain the status quo of inequality within the apartheid-scarred nation. But despite the tactics of the oppressive regime to derail Mandela's quest for equality for all of the citizens of South Africa, the African warrior stood his ground, held up by a fortress-like faith in Almighty God and the unflagging support of millions of freedom-loving South Africans who yearned for constructive changes within the fabric of the racially fractured nation. Because Mandela kept hope alive by enduring the hardships of the inhumane regime that was on the wrong side of history, on April 27, 1994, he became the first democratically elected president of all the people of South Africa.

Remaining Hopeful: Keeping an Open Heart

The ability to remain hopeful in those instances when we are assailed by life's difficulties is crucial as to whether pain, sorrow, deprivation, and all of the absurdities impacting our life situation will become part of our soul's stretching or shrinking. In other words, *embracing the conscious decision to become practitioners of hope in those instances when we are impacted by adversity is crucial as to whether or not we will survive or collapse under the pressure of the ordeal assaulting our lives.* History teaches us that liberation from painful experiences is contingent on both the emotional and spiritual responses we bring to bear on the absurdities that conspire to crack our lives open. Even though the heart is recognized as the organ designed by the Creator for pumping blood through the human body, it is frequently referred to in literature as the seat of emotions. As such, when we speak about emotional responses to life situations, we oftentimes refer to them as "heart responses."

A revealing insight ensuing from testimonials of individuals who were fortunate enough to survive difficult experiences reveal that our emotional response to adversity will either render us bitter or better. In those instances when we respond to difficulties with a heart of bitterness, we degrade our capacity to envision a transformed future, and we open ourselves up to being consumed by the bitterness we grant entry into our being. Bitterness poisons our emotions and degrades the energy that might be employed in devising carefully thought out strategies that could be used to help us address the difficulties impacting our lives. When we become consumed by bitterness, our ability to engage in critical thinking is also clouded. And we oftentimes foreclose on a more productive future because we relinquish our better judgment to the rule of the destructive emotion instead of employing carefully thought out strategies that could be instrumental in helping us address and resolve our crisis situation.

When we relinquish our self-control to life-limiting emotions such as bitterness, we fail to maintain the emotional poise that would enable us to critically access what is transpiring in our lives. Unable to do this, we are rendered incapable of mounting effective responses that could be beneficial in helping us resolve besetting problems. In such instances, adversity becomes a wall instead of a window through which we are able to envision new realities.

When this happens, a sense of malaise sets in, causing us to become absorbed in a self-indulgent state of gloom and feeling helpless about our situation. As time progresses, however, it proves to be a difficult task in shaking feelings of despondency, and we succumb to the state of helplessness laying siege to our being. In these times we are prime candidates for shutting down spiritually and emotionally, self-destructing in the downward spiral of self-defeating emotions that ensue from inefficient coping strategies that are birthed in a heart of bitterness. This lends credence to the fact that bitterness is an ineffective tool for resolving life's problems.

In those instances when we deny bitterness the opportunity to overwhelm us and choose instead to respond to difficulties with a heart of hope, the possibilities for liberation are unlimited. *By keeping the door of our heart oriented to new possibilities, we deny difficult experiences the opportunity to consign us to states of depression and despair.* Additionally, when we keep the door of our heart open to new possibilities, we avail ourselves to impartation from a source that is far more powerful than the difficulties that are impacting us—a source with power to sustain us through seasons of despair and despondency, thereby preventing us from becoming entrapped in life-withering emotions.

It matters not how bad any situation is, or how bad it might get, the choice ultimately remains ours as to whether or not we will choose to remain anchored in the providential care of Almighty God, or whether we will choose to surrender to oppressive forces that threaten to sabotage our sense of well-being. God works through an open heart and will tabernacle with us in the extremities of life when we keep the shutters of our heart open to the truth that He is predisposed to providing us with impartation capable of birthing new realities in our lives.

If we are honest with ourselves, we might admit that letting go of bitterness is no easy task. But you may recognize that a recurring theme in the teachings of Jesus is the principle of displacement. Just as the Old Testament tells us that our heavenly Father gives us beauty for ashes (see Isa. 61:3), Jesus similarly reminds us that in those instances when we relinquish death-dealing emotions, He replaces them with life-expanding ones, as evidenced by His teaching that the pure in heart *"will see God"* (Matt. 5:8 NRSV). In other words, when we strive to *"overcome evil with good"* (Rom. 12:21 NRSV), the Holy Spirit displaces that which is evil within us, replacing it with that which is good. When this happens, we are involved in an exchange transaction in which we receive something good from God—we become indwelt by the life-transforming power of Almighty God.

Remaining Hopeful: Keeping an Open Spirit

During seasons of adversity, life is fraught with pain and suffering and it becomes a herculean task to live fully in the moment. *Living fully in the moment necessitates the exercise of hope by laying claim to those things which faith has believed to be truly promised*

by God. While living with an attitude of expectancy involves entrusting emotional aspects of our being to the providential care of
Almighty God, it also entails keeping our spiritual circuits open
to the transformative power of the Holy Spirit. *When we keep
the circuits of our spirit open to receiving the inrushing energies of
Almighty God, we give the Holy Spirit the opportunity to give us
impartation that changes us and renders us strong, despite the fact
that our emotional well-being might not be all that we would like it
to be under periods of extreme duress.* Keeping the circuits of our
spirit open to the transformative power of the Holy Spirit calls for
remaining anchored on the truths enshrined in God's word re-
gardless of the way we might be *feeling* at any given point in time.

The architects of the apartheid regime on numerous occasions offered Nelson Mandela immediate release from prison if he
pled guilty to the charges of treason that were leveled against him,
in addition to promising that he would abandon the struggle to
dismantle the heartless apparatus of social engineering that prevented millions of South Africa's citizens from realizing their God-
given potential as complete human beings. Even though he was at
times emotionally despondent, he refused to give up the fight in
his spirit. He indicated that had he abandoned the struggle to attain equality for all of the citizens of South Africa, he would have
betrayed the core belief that apartheid was a sinister system that
robbed millions of black, Indian, and mixed-race South Africans
of their God-ordained status as full human beings, in addition to
being a crime against humanity. Armed with the conviction that
his struggle was a noble one, he spurned repeated entreaties of
the gatekeepers of the apartheid regime to have him recant his
beliefs, and kept "hoping against hope" for the dawning of a new
day when the waters of liberation would rush down like a healing
stream on the strife-torn nation and set its people free.

Writing in *Long Walk to Freedom*, Mandela tells about experiencing dark and despairing days when he was subjected to long stretches of solitary confinement that tested his resolve of remaining true to his life's mission—dismantling the dehumanizing apparatus of apartheid in his native South Africa. In addition to being subjected to long stretches of solitary confinement, his energy was constantly sapped and disillusionment colored his mental skies, because at no point in time was he ever absolutely certain about the general well-being of his beloved wife, children, and other family members residing beyond the confines of the massive prison walls. Employing every possible device to break the will of inmates, prison officials deliberately withheld mail from political prisoners—a strategy which Mandela admitted made his spirit feel as barren and dry as the great Karroo Desert covering hundreds of square miles of terrain within the borders of his native land. He indicated that in those instances, when his solitary lifeline to the outside world was severed, it necessitated that he plumb the unfathomable depths of his spirit in order to summon the resiliency and self-discipline that prevented him from exploding internally and losing hope.[6]

We live in an era of unsurpassed technology. And we are constantly being seduced by the tantalizing efficiency of electronic gadgets, and buy into the erroneous notion that changes in our life situation should materialize instantaneously. In a world that lunges for instant gratification, modern-day appliances have conditioned us to having our needs addressed with lightening speed, so much so, that the expectation of immediacy has permeated just about every facet of modern life. On account of this reality, we invariably opt for superficial answers that afford us hasty exits from life's besetting problems instead of recognizing that the stretch of adversity to which we are oftentimes subjected might very well be the means whereby God invites us to reflect on how well we are fulfilling our higher calling. In our haste to seek release from our pain-predicament, we fail to recognize that God is ultimately in control of our life circumstances and has the last word as to how our situation will turn out. When we cultivate the capacity to embrace this liberating insight, we become better predisposed to remaining still, listening to what the Holy Spirit is attempting to teach us in the midst of our season of adversity. Additionally, by assuming a posture of stillness, we also become predisposed to cultivating a sense of gratitude for the lesson of steadfastness that we become privy to while being compelled to rely on the providential care of Almighty God to bring about transformation in our life situation.

C.S. Lewis wrote, "God whispers to us in our pleasure, speaks to us in our conscience, but shouts in our pain: it is His megaphone to rouse a deaf world."[7] Pain is a human phenomenon that insists on being attended to rather than ignored. Art Lindsley writes, "Pain wakes us up, and makes us ask fundamental questions that we might not ask otherwise."[8] It is a symptom of a cause that may not be readily apparent. It compels us to look at our lives from a sharper angle so we can ascertain the root cause of our suffering. *Ultimately, it is the manner in which we choose to respond to the pain cascading across the terrain of our spirit that determines the state of mind with which we respond to life's dilemmas and emerge on the other side of the treadmill of trouble, transformed by a heightened sense of maturity.*

In addition to being a symbol of moral fortitude in the face of oppression, another hallmark of Nelson Mandela's life is the remarkable ability to refrain from being bitter. Nobel Peace Prize winner and Anglican Archbishop, Desmond Tutu, referred to his beloved friend and confidant as an "icon of forgiveness and reconciliation."[9] During his lengthy prison experience, Mandela cultivated the insight to recognize that the season of adversity to which he was subjected not only served to highlight the plight of blacks, Indians, and mixed-race South Africans who were being trampled under the oppressive heel of the nefarious regime, but it also provided the opportunity for the dawning of a new era in which a liberated nation could legislate laws that are congruent with the progressive policies of the civilized world. It additionally provided a climate that was conducive to the fostering of a spirit of collaboration and collegiality among the nation's diverse ethnic groups, enabling former adversaries the opportunity to pursue peace, and *"beat their swords into plowshares, and their spears into pruning hooks"* (Isa. 2:4 NRSV). Further still, it played a pivotal role in ending the nation's pariah status in the world community, which ensued from the policies of an indifferent regime that was out of touch with those of the civilized world.

Mandela's struggle highlighted the possibilities of the God of hope, because deep in his spirit he discerned a voice calling into history, declaring, "Behold, I make all things new." Because he chose to keep the frequencies of his spirit open to the vision of a new reality that was destined to materialize in his native land, Mandela cultivated the inner fortitude and spiritual stamina to resist the status quo. Because of his hope-filled orientation to the future, he courageously embraced the mantle as one of the spiritual midwives who played a pivotal role in birthing forces that were instrumental in dismantling the apparatus of apartheid that held millions of South Africans captive, thereby ushering in an era of freedom for all ethnic groups throughout the length and breadth of the liberated nation.

Keeping one's spirit open to the advent of new life while we are being impacted by the fiery ordeals of life is no easy task. And it is much more than uttering simplistic slogans, such as, "When the going gets tough, the tough get going." In those instances when we are subjected to the spirit-crushing volleys of adversity, we are oftentimes tempted to submit to the entreaties of revenge that entice us to even scores whenever possible. However, even though we might be impacted in negative ways by difficult experiences, God desires that we address adversity with constructive responses, and strive to keep the peace instead of keeping score. God in His infinite wisdom knows that genuflecting before the altar of revenge would ultimately give birth to a dynamic that generates additional episodes of suffering and pain, as stipulated by the *lex talionis* or "law of retaliation," voiced in many ancient cultures as "An eye for an eye and a tooth for a tooth," and whose dictum contains bitter seeds with the potential of rendering us blind and toothless. As such, our heavenly Father admonishes us to cultivate the spirit of forgiveness that prevents us from being consumed with settling of scores and focusing instead on the birthing of new realities that are possible through the exercise of faith.

God desires that we struggle with every fiber of our being to discover meaning in the midst of life's pain-predicaments, as indicated by Dr. Frankl, who said that "life holds a potential meaning under any conditions, even the most miserable ones."[10] God has mysterious ways of birthing new realities in our lives out of seemingly hopeless situations when we remain receptive to His entreaties to envision a transformed future. Cultivating the capacity to find meaning for our lives in those instances when we are confronted with difficult experiences can only become a reality when we exercise hope and keep our spiritual frequencies open to the dawning of new and glorious possibilities that are available to us when we entrust our circumstances to God's providential care.

The plight of Joseph, beginning in the 37th chapter of Genesis, reveals striking similarities to the contemporary life experience of Nelson Mandela. It also lends credence to the fact that even though the ability to keep our spirit oriented toward hope in those instances when we are immersed in the floodwaters of adversity is no easy task—but it is by no means fanciful. Both individuals cultivated the capacity to struggle for redemption and renewal while consigned to the school of hard knocks, and both emerged from their pain-predicament unencumbered by feelings of bitterness.

Joseph was the youngest and favorite son of Israel, a wealthy landowner and father of the patriarchs after whom the 12 tribes of Israel were named. Because of the spiritual gift of dreaming and interpreting dreams, he unfortunately ignited the ire of his jealous brothers, who perpetrated a crime that was punishable by death under Hebrew religious law (see Exod. 21:16), when they kidnapped their 17-year-old sibling and maliciously sold him for 20 pieces of silver to a band of Ishmaelite slave traders travelling from Gilead with camels loaded with spices and balm. And it was they who transported him across the border into Egypt where they resold him as a slave.

After being stripped of his sense of personhood and sold into slavery by individuals trafficking in human beings, Joseph became the property of Potiphar, a powerful Egyptian army general who was captain of the guard, and who had oversight of Pharaoh's prison system. After taking careful note of Joseph's work ethic during the time he was consigned to his jurisdiction, Potiphar recognized that the young man possessed exemplary skills that could be beneficial to his administration. Armed with this information,

Potiphar accorded Joseph the heavy responsibility as overseer of his household.

In addition to exemplary skills, the Creator endowed Joseph with matinee idol looks. After being smitten by his good looks, Potiphar's wife began making sexual advances toward the handsome youth. One day, when Potiphar was away from home, his wife attempted to seduce Joseph. Frightened by the prospect of what could happen to him if he opted to engage in a romp in the hay with his boss's wife, Joseph ran from her room while she desperately struggled to get him into bed with her. During the attempt to break free from her clutches, Potiphar's wife grabbed hold of his tunic and stripped it off of his body. Angry and insulted over the fact that she could not have her way with the handsome young man, the spurned aggressor became furious and vindictively accused Joseph of attempted rape to members of the unsuspecting household staff, simultaneously brandishing as "evidence" the clothing that he ran off and supposedly left in her hands.

When Potiphar arrived home later that very evening, the conniving seductress relayed the well-rehearsed fabricated story to her husband that she presented to the unsuspecting household staff earlier in the day. Potiphar became furious over the disturbing report and stipulated that Joseph be remanded to prison. However, there is a strong possibility that the general might have had some reservations about his wife's morality and was probably more embarrassed than upset over the bogus report. In an attempt to save face, he possibly feigned being upset with Joseph and ordered the young man remanded to prison instead of having him executed. Whatever transpired in Potiphar's mind, influencing him to settle on the option that he finally did, it is quite evident that God worked mysteriously behind the scenes on Joseph's behalf.

At one point during his season of incarceration, Joseph interpreted the dream of the Pharaoh's butler, who, grateful for his help, promised that he would put in a good word to the king on the young man's behalf after he was released from prison. Unfortunately, after gaining his freedom, the emancipated butler soon forgot about the promises that were made to the young Hebrew who played a pivotal role in saving his life and orchestrating his release from prison. Despite the injustice and forgotten promises, God engineered Joseph's circumstances, elevating him to the position of prime minister over the Egyptian empire.

In response to a query from the Pharaoh concerning a troubling dream that he experienced, Joseph warned the king of the advent of seven years of bountiful harvests that would immediately be followed by seven years of harsh famine. Recognizing that the Creator endowed Joseph with supernatural insight, the Pharaoh assigned him the heavy responsibility of stockpiling grain for the inevitable disaster that he predicted would materialize at a future date. Meanwhile, back in Israel, Joseph's family was subjected to the ravages of famine that gripped the entire Middle Eastern region during the season of scarcity. In order to prevent starvation from decimating his household, Israel dispatched Joseph's brothers to Egypt to purchase grain for his family, totally unaware of the fact that his young son was the astute mastermind who was orchestrating the massive food distribution system that was currently operating in the land of the pharaohs.

When Joseph's siblings arrived in Egypt, he immediately recognized them. But instead of readily welcoming his estranged brethren with open arms, he deliberately became cagey, and refrained from revealing his true identity. After an extended interval of game playing, he finally relented and made himself known to the awe-struck kidnappers. Joseph later became aware of the fact that his brothers were concerned that he might exact retribution against them for having sold him into slavery. In a gesture of forgiveness, he assuaged their anxieties, saying, *"Even though you intended to do harm to me, God intended it for good, in order to preserve a numerous people, as He is doing today"* (Gen. 50:20 NRSV). Joseph's response to his brothers signified that God's divine will could never be thwarted by human design, despite the depth of human perversity.

Joseph was a youthful 30-year-old when Pharaoh elevated him to the powerful office of prime minister over Egypt. After 13 years of unimaginable anguish and humiliation while consigned to a prison house of pain and privation, he cultivated the capacity to discern that instead of allowing the difficulties impacting his life situation to render his spirit bitter and brittle, there was a positive way of responding to adversity. Because he kept his spirit open to the providential care of Almighty God, and because he exercised hope for a new reality, he was entrusted with the divine assignment of rescuing not only the citizens of Egypt and neighboring territories from imminent starvation, but also the very individuals that conspired to do him harm. Instead of responding to adversity with a spirit of bitterness, he learned the important lesson that suffering was something to be dealt with, lived through, learned from, and redeemed. Armed with liberating insight that was seeded into his spirit by Almighty God, Joseph cultivated the inner fortitude to endure hardship, and looked past the predicament in which he was immersed in order to reap the fruits of redemption and renewal that are possible through faith in Almighty God. He recognized that the eye of faith enables us to visualize an alternate reality inside the immediacy of life's most difficult situations. Because he remained resolute in cultivating a spirit that was unencumbered by bitterness or revenge, God utilized the trusting soul as a tributary of grace to inaugurate His divine plan on the world stage.

The life experiences of Nelson Mandela and Joseph are proof positive that there are life-transforming potentials embedded in the most horrific pain-predicament. The late British Prime Minister, Winston Churchill, purportedly stated, *"In every difficulty there is an equivalent seed of equal or greater benefit."* As such, when we purpose to keep our spirit unencumbered by bitterness and look to God for the birthing of new realities in our life situation, we afford our heavenly Father the opportunity to fashion us a new future.

Nelson Mandela and Joseph were presented with every plausible reason as to why they should distill their frustrations into a core of bitterness and resentment. But instead of cursing the darkness and allowing the seasons of adversity impacting their lives to shrink their spirit into inner, private hells, both individuals recognized the wisdom of employing the difficult seasons to which they were relegated as opportunities to entrust their circumstances to the providential care of Almighty God. The orientation to the future adopted by both individuals served to radicalize their perspective on life, thus altering their identities. Both persevered in keeping hope alive, employing it as a catalyst that emboldened and deepened their faith in the unlimited possibilities of the Creator.

Like hope, faith is numbered among the three theological virtues (see 1 Cor. 13:11) and it is also recognized as one of the seven fruits of the Spirit (see Gal. 5:22). It is the next rung on the ladder we are exhorted to grab hold of as we migrate from difficult experiences to the threshold of God's glorious liberation.

Reflection Questions

1. Do you consider yourself to be a practitioner of hope? Why?

2. In what ways do you employ hope as a means of envisioning a transformed future?

3. What biblical evidence supports your premise for remaining hopeful in light of the difficulties that confront you on a daily basis?

CHAPTER FOUR

Keep Faith Alive in Difficult Times

Throughout the history of the Church, faith has served as an agent for transmitting doctrine and sustaining the vision of believers. It is an attitude of the spirit, and the axle around which the lives of God's children revolve. Faith is also the foundation stone on which the future outlook of believers is erected.

Percy C. Ainsworth argues that faith is the constant factor in life's spiritual reckonings, and one of the timeless words in earth's vocabulary. For its deep roots and wide range, there is nothing like unto it in the wide sweep of the eternal.[1] Jesus indicated that if we possessed faith as small as a grain of mustard seed, we would be able to move mountains (see Matt. 17:20). In His reference to size, Jesus intimated that in those instances when we demonstrate the tiniest amount of faith in God, we open ourselves up to experiencing unlimited possibilities in our lives. However, before we could employ faith as an agent to effectuate transformation of our life situation, we must acquire a firm understanding of what faith really is.

Faith is a term that is frequently invoked in both the secular and religious spheres of life. Unfortunately, in far too many instances it is utilized as nothing more than a pious platitude, lacking the power to bring about transformation in the lives of God's children, which is what it is supposed to do. The writer of Hebrews states: *"And without faith it is impossible to please God, for whoever would approach Him must believe that He exists and that He rewards those who seek Him"* (Heb. 11:6 NRSV). The writer supports his premise by referencing a roll call of biblical luminaries that Scripture identifies as exemplars of faith—Barak, Sampson, Jephthah, David, and Samuel the prophet—who through faith were able to conquer kingdoms, enforce justice, receive promises, stop the mouth of lions, quench raging fires, escape the edge of the sword, win strength out of weakness, become mighty in war, put armies to flight, and experience the resurrection of loved ones back from the dead (see Heb. 11:32-34).

Both of these references lend credence to the fact that not only are we given the opportunity to align our wills with God's will through the exercise of faith, we are also afforded access to a source of power capable of transforming our life situation. In other words, through the exercise of faith we are given the opportunity to approximate the divine blueprint for our lives when we entrust our circumstances to the providential care of God. Through the exercise of faith we avail ourselves to transformation by power ensuing from a supernatural source lying beyond the sphere of our limited understanding. This power is nothing more than the life of God operating through our members and transforming us into the Creator's divine specifications.

Faith: Collaborating With Hope

Faith does not operate as an independent entity. It works in a collaborative effort with hope to engender the transformation of our life situation, because it is through hope that we are able to appropriate those things which faith believes to have been promised by God. While faith believes that God is true to His word, hope awaits the time when the reality of God will be manifested in our lives. Faith believes that according to the teachings of the Bible, God is a benevolent Father who has the welfare of His children as His highest priority and is actively involved in shaping their destiny.

Hope expects that, with the unfolding of time, God will reveal Himself as Father to His children. Through the exercise of faith, we also believe that eternal life is the spiritual birthright of every human being. But even though we might view life through "a glass darkly" (see 1 Cor. 13:12), hope anticipates that at some future date the full revelation of God will be disclosed to us in a more meaningful way. In other words, hope is the scaffolding on which faith is erected.

Faith could not operate without hope, because hope provides support and sustenance to faith. Hope is the agent that energizes faith to work toward birthing new realities in our life situation. Even though knowledge of Christ becomes possible through faith, without hope faith will falter and knowledge will become nothing more than a pipe dream. Without faith, hope loses its efficacy and is rendered a dead faith. While faith in Christ provides hope with its assurance, hope endues faith with vitality, pointing us to future horizons that offer new life.

Belief Is an Indispensible Component of Faith

Scripture indicates that faith and belief are inseparable allies that work in a collaborative effort to accomplish transformation in the lives of believers. The biblical record indicates that in order to access God through the exercise of faith, we must believe that He exists (see Heb. 11:6). Many people confuse belief as the same thing as faith, but there is a distinct difference. Even though some people claim to believe in the existence of God, they unfortunately lack personal faith in Him. In very much the same way that someone might believe that an aircraft is mechanically sound enough to execute a safe flight from one destination to another, they might still lack the faith to take a flight aboard the aircraft as a passenger.

Belief is the conviction that God is a living entity that is capable of accomplishing the transformation of our life situation. Therefore, belief working in a collaborative effort with faith enables us to entrust our circumstances to God. Writing to Timothy, his spiritual son in the ministry, the apostle Paul declared: *"But I am not ashamed, for I **know** the One in whom I have put my trust, and I am sure that He is able to guard until that day what I have entrusted to Him"* (2 Tim. 1:12 NRSV). The apostle Paul was an individual whose faith undergirded his belief that God's word is true and could be relied upon. Faith gave life to Paul's belief system, making it possible for him to act on his belief.

After His transfiguration on the Mount of Transfiguration in the presence of Peter, James, and John—the three disciples frequently referred to by theologians as the members of his "inner cabinet"—Jesus returned to base camp at which point He was confronted by a distraught father who presented his son to the disciples remaining at the foot of the mountain, requesting that they cast a dumb spirit out of the young man. Repeated attempts on the part of the disciples to provide healing to the youth proved unsuccessful, prompting his father to turn to the leader of the pack for help. After presenting his son to Jesus, the Lord questioned the petitioner as to whether or not he believed in His ability to cast the demon out of his son. The father responded, saying: *"I believe;* ***help*** *my unbelief!"* (Mark 9:24 NRSV).

The man and his entire family were enmeshed in anguish over the fact that a malevolent emissary of Satan desperately sought to destroy their family member. But before any transformation could be forthcoming in the young man's situation, his father was required to demonstrate his belief in Jesus's ability to cast the evil spirit out of his son. In other words, he was required to activate his faith and trust Jesus implicitly. By so doing, he would entertain absolutely no doubt in his mind that Jesus possessed the ability to heal his son.

In a letter to the church at Philippi, the apostle Paul encouraged saints at that location to *"work out your own salvation with fear and trembling; for it is God who is at work in you, enabling you both to will and to work for **His** good pleasure"* (Phil. 2:12-13 NRSV). While it might appear that the resolution to life's problems is wholly contingent on our "working out our salvation," the Bible indicates that God, by His good will, works through us to make our petitions a reality in our lives when we exercise faith in His providence. Even though the final outcome is not entirely dependent on us, God's promises could only be manifested in our lives when we believe them to be true and augment our belief by unfurling our faith and trusting Him implicitly. In other words, we cannot experience the manifestation of a reality that we do not fully embrace through the exercise of faith. When Jesus requested that the father believe in His ability to heal his son, He was indicating that change could only manifest itself in our individual life situation when we expect that our heavenly Father will accomplish those things which we believe are possible through the exercise of faith.

Matthew's rendering of the incident tells us that after Jesus healed the young man, the befuddled disciples questioned the Master concerning their inability to cast the evil spirit out of him. Jesus informed them that they were unable to do this because of their unbelief (see Matt. 17:20). He further added: *"Howbeit this kind goeth out but by prayer and fasting"* (Matt. 17:21). Jesus's reference to *"this kind"* implied the existence of different degrees of demonic activity that are operative in the spiritual realm, indicating that the application of different levels of spiritual power are needed to cast them out.

By drawing attention to the unreliability of the belief system of the disciples, Jesus highlighted the fact that they were incapable of defeating certain levels of demonic activity. While the disciples harbored no doubts about Jesus's ability to accomplish the impossible, their own abilities were hamstrung by unbelief because they lost the power that was entrusted to them when He gave them authority over *all* levels of demonic activity (see Matt. 10:8-18). On account of their unbelief, God's possibilities could no longer be fully manifested in their lives. And this was contingent on the fact that they failed to reconstitute their divine energies through the practice of fasting and prayer.

Scripture is populated with instances where Jesus separated Himself from His disciples to engage in periods of fasting and prayer. And it was through fasting and prayer that He opened up His being to the transforming power of the Holy Spirit, thereby reconstituting His spiritual power on a daily basis. This truth prompted the apostle Paul to state that *"in* [Jesus] *dwelleth all the fullness of the Godhead bodily"* (Col. 2:9). Because the disciples of Jesus failed to reconstitute their spiritual power through the practice of fasting and prayer, they were no longer able to exercise the authority Jesus had given them before they became inflicted with the spiritual anemia that ensued. In lieu of this reality, they frequently engaged in empty rituals, working from accumulated knowledge rather than a fresh connection with God. They were men with an emerging faith and were frequently referred to by Jesus as men of "little faith" (see Matt. 8:26), indicating that they were "on the way" to developing a deeper faith in the Almighty.

In order for God's power to be manifested in the life of the youth, Jesus requested that the father's belief in His ability to heal the young man approximate unswerving faith in His heavenly Father's ability to accomplish the impossible; just like Abraham believed God and his belief was counted for righteousness (see Gal. 2:6). The father was required to take a quantum leap of faith and visualize his son in a state of wholesomeness as God saw him. He was required to demonstrate the faith *of* God, with absolutely no reservations whatsoever that the Almighty would restore the health of his son. By exercising the faith of God and visualizing his son in a perfect state of health as God saw him, the vision of full health became God's gift to him. By activating his faith and trusting Jesus to do the impossible, he was able to "see" with his spiritual eyes what he could not see with his physical eyes. And what he envisioned with his spiritual eyes became his gift from God.

Trust Is Indispensible to Belief

Trust is the vehicle that transports us to environs beyond the realm of belief. When we believe in someone or something, we feel confident enough to entrust our circumstances to that person or thing with absolutely no reservations whatsoever. It could be said that our relationship with our heavenly Father is ultimately reduced to the element of trust. This is corroborated by the sentiments of the prophet Isaiah, who declared: *"Thou wilt keep him in perfect peace, whose mind is stayed on Thee, because he trusted in Thee"* (Isa. 26:3).

In the face of deep suffering, it is not uncommon for us to become challenged in the area of our faith. Challenges to our faith oftentimes cause us to buy into victim status and embrace the illusion that we've been abandoned by God. In those instances when we are standing at Ground Zero of adversity, we are prone to feel cast adrift from the unconditional love of the Eternal One, influencing us to entertain thoughts that He might have abdicated His protective watch over the universe. This sentiment is echoed in the psalmist's lament of dereliction on the occasion when he demonstrated feelings of abandonment on the part of God: *"Why standest Thou afar off, O Lord? Why hidest Thou Thyself in times of trouble?"* (Ps. 10:1). This mindset causes our trust in God's providential care to waver, enticing us to embrace the belief that in the final analysis God might not have our best interests at heart after all. If the truth be told, however, God is head over heels in love with His creation and will *never* abandon us. This sentiment is echoed in the affirmation of the psalmist's cry of declaration: *"Lord, You have been our dwelling place in all generations"* (Ps. 90:1 NRSV).

The Book of First Kings chronicles the exploits of the prophet Elijah, someone the Bible recognizes as one of the exemplars of biblical faith. After praying to God, the Creator responded to His servant's petition to withhold rain from falling throughout Israel for three years. On a subsequent occasion, Elijah was engaged in a contest on Mount Carmel with the prophets of Baal to ascertain whether the Canaanite god Baal or the God of Israel was the sovereign ruler over the universe.

On the occasion of the contest, Elijah petitioned God for another request. God responded to His prophet's petition and rained fire down from heaven, consuming the sacrifice on the altar he had erected as well as the water in the trench surrounding the altar. At the cessation of the pyrotechnic display, Elijah instructed the spectators on the mountain to seize all 250 prophets of Baal. After being seized, they were taken to the brook of Kishon, where Elijah executed each of them with a sword. After Jezebel, wife of king Ahab and prophetess of Baal, received word that Elijah had executed the pagan prophets, she became furious and dispatched a messenger of doom to Elijah, informing him that by the very hour on the following day, he would likewise be subjected to the fate that he dispensed to her disciples. Staring at the prospects confronting him, Elijah became consumed by fear and fled for his life. He was so traumatized by despair that he embarked on a day's journey into the wilderness, where he reposed under a juniper tree and wished death upon himself. During his season of despair, an angel of the Lord appeared on the desert scene and provided nourishment to the distraught prophet. After Elijah regained his strength, the angel led him to a cave up in the higher elevations of Mount Horeb, where he conversed with the Lord. Scripture tells us that Elijah stood on the mountain waiting (see 1 Kings 19:11).

*And he said, Go forth, and stand upon the mount before
the Lord. And, behold, the Lord passed by, and a great and
strong wind rent the mountains, and brake in pieces the
rocks before the Lord; but the Lord was not in the wind:
and after the wind an earthquake; but the Lord was not
in the earthquake: and after the earthquake a fire; but the
Lord was not in the fire: and after the fire a still small voice*
(1 Kings 19:11-12).

The voice was that of God providing assurance to Elijah that no power on earth was powerful enough to snatch him from the protective custody of God's providential care.

Elijah was entrusted with the responsibility of ridding the nation of Israel of its hankering after Baal, whose cultic practices Ahab and Jezebel instituted as the court religion of Israel after abandoning the worship of Jehovah. Throughout the years of his ministry, Elijah was committed to the leadership of the Holy Spirit that enabled the Almighty to honor his petition of withholding rain from falling throughout Israel, and raining fire down from heaven on Mount Carmel. However, on the occasion when he was confronted with adversity that threatened his longevity, he lost confidence in God's providential care and behaved the way countless scores of humans do when they are confronted with life-threatening circumstances. He assumed that God had abandoned him. Instead of choosing to remain anchored in the providential care of his Maker, the threat of Jezebel's sword reversed the flow of his faith, causing it to waiver to the point where fear and defeat were able to control him.

Writing in *Worship as David Lived It*, Judson Cornwall said, "Fear and faith are exactly the same energy running in opposite directions. 'Faith' says, I believe in God, and 'fear' says I believe the enemy. 'Faith' says that God's promises will be fulfilled, but 'fear' declares that the enemy's threats will be realized."[2] Elijah temporarily lost trust in the providential care of the Creator, causing his faith to be reversed to fear. He became so overwhelmed by the difficulties confronting him that instead of remaining anchored in the providence of Almighty God, he chose to surrender to fear. He unfortunately focused on how big the problem confronting him was instead of focusing on how big God is. By so doing, he allowed his spirit to be invaded by fear and defeat, causing him to lose trust in the all-sufficiency of Almighty God.

After being reconstituted with spiritual power that enabled him to realign his belief to the truth that he could entrust his circumstances to the providential care of Almighty God, Elijah abandoned his defeatist attitude and began living once again from the source of power that fueled his prophetic mission. Even though he was subjected to an isolated episode of failure, his legacy lends credence to a ministry that was overwhelmingly rooted in the all-sufficiency of Almighty God. As such, God honored Elijah's legacy, sparing him the experience of death, and translated him directly to the courts of Jehovah in the confines of a fiery chariot (see 2 Kings 2).

Elijah's legacy was held in such high esteem by his successor, Elisha, that when the old prophet questioned his young protégé as to what request he would have him fulfill before he embarked on his initiation into eternity, Elisha indicated that he was desirous of being endowed with a double portion of the spirit that permeated the life of Elijah. After Elijah departed the earthly plane, Elisha assumed leadership of the school of the prophets. Elisha's legacy bears witness to the fact that he was granted the request of being endowed with a double portion of the very spirit that permeated the life of his mentor and predecessor, Elijah.

Faith Is a Spiritual Kernel Deposited in the Human Spirit by God

The Bible tells us that God endows each life with a measure of faith (see Rom. 12:3). In other words, faith is a spiritual kernel deposited in the human spirit during the creative process. It is a seed whose maturity each individual is responsible for nurturing to access the source that avails us power for the living of our days. While it is impossible to quantitatively ascertain the faith content of individuals by employing man-made instruments, it is quite evident that some people are more successful than others at enhancing their life situation because they are more inclined than others to nurturing the measure of faith that has been deposited in their spirit by the Creator. Individuals demonstrating the inclination to maximize the measure of faith that has been entrusted to them by the Creator are frequently referred to as people of "big faith." However, the fact that so-called people with "big faith" are more inclined to enhance their life situation than people with "little faith" does not mean that people with "big faith" are endowed with a larger measure than the rest. It simply means that they work in a collaborative effort with GOD much better than individuals displaying "little faith," because they tend to entrust their circumstances to the providential care of Almighty God as opposed to others who are ambivalent about entrusting their circumstances to God's providential care.

Percy C. Ainsworth indicates that only the faith that can trust God at *all* times can trust Him at *any* time. The renowned theologian believes that the moment faith heeds the dictation of circumstances, it ceases to be faith and becomes calculation. He indicates that all faith is transcendent and independent of the conditions in which it has to live. It is not snared in the strange web of the tentative and experimental. And whoever has for one moment felt the power of faith has gone beyond the dominion of time.[3]

Corroborating the sentiments of Ainsworth, the Reverend Dr. Martin Luther King Jr. invoked the words of French philosopher and theologian, Gabriel Marcel, who indicated that faith is *believing in* instead of *believing that*. He continues, it is "opening a credit; which puts me at the disposal of the one whom I believe." When I believe, states Marcel, "I rally to with that sort of interior gathering of oneself which the act of rallying implies." Faith, in Dr. King's estimation, is the opening of all sides and at every level of one's life to the divine inflow.[4]

The fact that people with "big faith" entrust their circumstances implicitly to the providential care of Almighty God despite the difficult circumstances in which they are immersed reflects the *nature* of their faith and not the measure of it. Invariably, these individuals focus on the acquisition of the life of God. Through faith, they strive to make the Eternal One the highest dimension of their existence instead of merely seeking to extract material blessings from Him.

The primary objective of people with "big faith" is the attainment of mystical union with God. It is the *nature* of their response to difficulties that result in transformation of their circumstances. This lends credence to the fact that when we open ourselves up to the quickening power of the Holy Spirit, the more latitude we afford God to transform our life situation. And the more access the life of God is afforded into the corridors of our spirit, the greater freedom God is afforded to shape us according to His specifications as mutual collaboration occurs between the human spirit and the Holy Spirit in bringing about the transformation of our life circumstances. The kingdom of God in Jesus's teaching points to the manifest assertion of God's loving and righteous rule.

David is a prime example of someone who demonstrated the ardent desire of wanting more of God instead of merely seeking to acquire material gifts. Israel's favorite son declared: *"O God, Thou art my God; early will I seek Thee: my soul thirsteth for Thee, my flesh longeth for Thee in a dry and thirsty land, where no water is"* (Ps. 63:1-2). David did not center his affections exclusively on the acquisition of material blessings from God; his primary objective in life entailed being immersed in the personality of God, whereby he might be transformed into the Creator's image and likeness. As a result of this orientation to life, his surrender to the providential care of God made it possible for him to become a beneficiary of the Creator's blessings.

The teachings of Jesus indicate that the blessings we accrue to ourselves are contingent on the nature of faith we employ in accessing impartation from God. The Supreme Teacher declared: *"According to your faith be it unto you"* (Matt. 9:29). In other words, God's response to our petitions is contingent on the nature of faith we employ in living our lives. If we rely on God to manifest Himself in our lives and employ the nature of faith that unconditionally trusts in His ability to accomplish that which we ask of Him, He works *through* our spirit to accomplish far more than we could ever ask or imagine (see Eph. 3:20). The apostle Paul highlights the reality of God working through us as mystical union with Christ, where we are in Christ just as Christ is in us.

When we employ the nature of faith that believes God will do for us that which we ask of Him, the Holy Spirit works through our spirit, giving life to our beliefs, and making them a reality in our lives. Far too many people experience difficulty receiving blessings from God because even though they petition Him with their lips, they do not believe He will grant them the desires of their heart. As such, they fail to employ the nature of faith that believes God will grant them the desires of their heart. Ultimately, what they receive from God is contingent on the nature of their belief.

The writer of Hebrews tells us, *"Now faith is the substance of things hoped for, the evidence of things not seen"* (Heb. 11:1). In other words, it is the conviction of something envisioned in the invisible realm being brought into manifestation in the visible realm. Through the power of conviction, where we trust God implicitly, the Creator works on behalf of His children to bring into manifestation into the visible realm the realities that were conceptualized in the invisible realm. All of life's great inventions were conceptual ideas in the minds of their creators before they were birthed into concrete form in the material realm. When we act on the truth of what we know about God as outlined in the Bible, He transforms our life situation by providing us with impartation, enabling us to experience the manifestation of ideas that were conceptualized in the invisible realm, then becoming reality in the visible realm.

The apostle Paul encourages followers of Jesus to cultivate the same mind as Christ (see 1 Cor. 2:16), because it is through the exercise of Christlike faith that we acquire the worldview of the Savior. Jesus indicated that He and His Father are one (see John 10:30). Because of this, we appropriate the mind of Christ by trusting implicitly in the Master's word. And the unwavering belief in God's ability to meet our every need is the key that opens up our spirit to the inflow of the Holy Spirit so that we might receive impartation of divine energies from our heavenly Father.

By receiving impartation from God, we become imbued with the very faith of God, because impartation from our heavenly Father facilitates the co-mingling of the human spirit with the Holy Spirit, enabling us to share and reflect His nature. The faith of God becoming operative in the human spirit renders us as centers of *zoe*—spiritual life which is in God from all eternity—and the means by which we become empowered to experience transformation of life conditions that are congruent with God's *shalom*—His all-around goodness and harmony for His creation.

Access to Divine Life Through Faith Is the Birthright of Human Beings

Far too many people allow themselves to be relegated to life-withering conditions because they embrace the mistaken assumption that some limitation confronting them is their God-ordained lot in life. In other words, they operate on limiting beliefs about what God truly has in store for them. Writing in the Book of Acts, Luke records for us: *"For in Him we live, and move, and have our being"* (Acts 17:28). Luke's affirmation lends credence to the truth that access to the Holy Spirit is the spiritual birthright of every human being, because we live from a far more profound source when our lives are rooted in God. Living in ignorance of the truth that our existence ensues exclusively from the Spirit of God results in far too many people remaining cut off from *zoe*—true life. The refusal to draw succor and sustenance from the source of all life is the root of spiritual impoverishment in all of its varied guises. God desires that we partake of *shalom*—His all-around goodness and harmony for our lives, where nothing is broken or missing. And this only becomes possible when we are nurtured by power that emanates from God. Writing in *Mere Christianity*, C.S. Lewis declares: "Now God designed the human machine to run on Himself. He Himself is the fuel our spirits were designed to burn, or the food our spirits were designed to feed on. There is no other."[5]

And Jesus declared, *"I came that they may have life, and have it abundantly"* (John 10:10 NRSV). Due in large part to ignorance of the truth encapsulated in our Lord's proclamation, far too many people consign themselves to situations of hopelessness, limitation, and poverty because they are ignorant of the fact that they need never acquiesce to life-limiting conditions in any of their varied guises. There is no defeat, hopelessness, or limitation in God's economy. These conditions ensue from our refusal to access the divine source and fully partake of God's abundant life. Scripture exhorts us: *"Ask, and it will be given you; search, and you will find; knock, and the door will be opened for you"* (Matt. 7:7 NRSV). God is eternally predisposed to granting His children the desires of their heart. However, acquisition of our heavenly Father's gifts could only become a reality in our lives when through faith we ask, seek, and knock.

The Bible tells us that *"God is spirit, and those who worship Him must worship in spirit and truth"* (John 4:24 NRSV). Access to the possibilities of God is realized through the agency of the human spirit by the exercise of faith. Jesus informs us that the kingdom of God is resident *within* us, i.e. within the human spirit (see Luke 17:21). And it is through our spiritual orientation that we swing wide the portals of our being to the invasive rush of the Holy Spirit so we might become repositories of divine activity. Writing in the Book of Acts, Luke reminds us of Jesus's exhortation: *"But you will receive power when the Holy Spirit has come upon you"* (Acts 1:8 NRSV). When we activate with no reservations whatsoever the measure of faith which God has deposited in our spirit by believing implicitly in His ability to accomplish that which we ask of Him, our spiritual accent becomes the key that unlocks the spiritual storehouse of heaven, affording the Holy Spirit unimpeded access to His earthly temples, transforming our life situation, and granting us our heart's desire.

While God does not necessarily listen to the petitions of our lips, He takes careful note of the nature of faith that is operative in our spirit. Oftentimes, what we declare with our lips during prayer amounts to nothing more than meaningless phrases that are uttered in parrot-fashion and inconsistent with the belief that is resident in our spirit. In such instances, we fail to obtain desired requests to prayer because the state of non-belief that pervades our spirit is unable to work with the Spirit of God. On account of this reality, the channels of our spirit become saturated by unbelief. We end up only receiving from God that which we truly believe He is able to accomplish in our lives, indicating that faith is the spiritual conviction about a certain reality. This truth is corroborated in the writing of James, when he makes the statement:

> *But let him ask in faith, nothing wavering. For he that wavereth is like a wave of the sea driven with the wind and tossed. For let not that man think that he shall receive any thing of the Lord. A double minded man is unstable in all his ways* (James 1:6-8).

Unbelief is doubt of God's omnipotence and of His faithfulness (see Rom. 4:20). Unbelief does not give God the opportunity to let God be God, because it doubts the dependability of a God who guarantees His promises. God is desirous that His children live as recipients of the very best that He has to offer us. Jesus affirmed this truth when He declared: *"Fear not, little flock; for it is your Father's good pleasure to give you the kingdom"* (Luke 12:32). This is proof positive that God created us as heirs of His very best. However, He could only give to us that which we are prepared to receive through the exercise of faith. Our heavenly Father is predisposed to bestowing blessings on every individual. Unfortunately, we frequently fail to appropriate His blessings to ourselves because the conduit between the human spirit and the Holy Spirit is blocked by unbelief, making it impossible for God's blessings to find a true home in His earthly temples.

Writing in the Book of First John, the apostle declares: *"Herein is love, not that we loved God, but that He loved us, and sent His Son to be the propitiation for our sins"* (1 John 4:10). Scripture is clear concerning the fact that God has the welfare of His creation as His highest priority, and that He is eternally predisposed to dispensing gifts to His children. Unfortunately, ignorance of this truth prevents scores of needy people from cultivating the capacity to partner with God in bestowing blessings upon them. Because of an impoverished worldview, they envision a limited God instead of visualizing Jehovah *El Shaddai*—Almighty God, Creator of the heavens and the earth.

Ignorance of the true personality of God in those instances when we are traumatized by the trials of life tend to exacerbate our pain-predicament, because in such instances we are inclined to fall prey to helplessness, hopelessness, and lovelessness, remaining estranged from the love of our lives. During seasons of adversity, we are prone to become blind to the fact that there is a source to which we could turn to obtain succor for the living of our days. This source is God Almighty. But failure to turn to God leaves us mired in our pain-predicament until such a time that we act on the truth that His liberating power is available to every soul at any time, and that He is predisposed to the transformation of all aspects of our existence. Because God truly has our welfare at heart, He tabernacles with us in whatever condition we might find ourselves, indicating that access to His storehouse of blessing is our divine birthright.

Access to the Mind of God Is Made Possible by Abiding in God

In the estimation of skeptics, we might be stretching things a bit by declaring that we are created with the capacity to receive impartation from the mind of God. Paul Tillich contends that "Man is man because he is created to receive a word from the dimension of the eternal."[6] Jesus indicated that He and His Father are one (see John 10:30). On account of this reality, we can become acquainted with the mind of God by abiding in or being formed by the teachings of Jesus.

Our Lord declared: *"If ye abide in Me, and My words abide in you, ye shall ask what ye will, and it shall be done unto you"* (John 15:7). From a spiritual point of view, abiding in Jesus is an inward turn whereby followers of the Nazarene discover their true identity, because it is through the act of abiding that we partake of God's divine nature. As we experience the resurrection life of Jesus that is made possible through God's divine energies, our own lives become transformed. In the words of the apostle Paul, abiding in Christ signifies that it is no longer we who live, but Christ who lives in us (see Gal. 2:20). That means that Christian living entails much more than the cognitive affirmation of biblical truths. It requires a personal appropriation of them. And the appropriation of God's truth consists of two key elements: love and obedience, which is evidenced by Jesus's declaration to His disciples: *"As the Father has loved Me, so I have loved you; abide in My love. If you keep My commandments, you will abide in My love, just as I have kept My Father's commandments and abide in His love"* (John 15:9-10 NRSV). Obedience to Jesus's commands is at the very heart of spiritual formation.

During His life on earth, Jesus was able to reflect the true stamp and imprimatur of the Godhead because the objective of His life mission entailed that of living in submission to the sovereignty of His heavenly Father's will (see Luke 2:49). And He attained this objective by drawing sustenance from the life of God.

Each soul is a potential channel through which God might express Himself. The created purpose of human beings is to express the image and likeness of God in a similar manner as Jesus, who envisioned Himself as the embodiment of the light of the world—the illumination or reflection of the Godhead. The Teacher always sought to impress upon the minds of His disciples that the spiritual pilgrimage of every human soul entails that of living as a potential agent of transformation and illumination of God—the salt of the earth and the light of the world (see Matt. 5:13-16).

During bouts of hardship, we are often influenced to look to sources other than God for resolution to the difficulties confronting us on this side of glory. We are prone to become impatient of waiting on our heavenly Father for liberation, and unwittingly surrender to life-shrinking forces that hold us in thrall instead of entrusting our circumstances to the providence of the Almighty, affording Him the opportunity to form His personality within us. God has our best interests at heart. And in order to facilitate our spiritual transformation, He oftentimes recognizes the need to subject us to painful experiences in order that we might learn the important lesson of abiding *in* Him. However, the painful experiences we are subjected to are not necessarily penal but transformational. Physicians frequently utilize medical alcohol to clean patients' wounds. While the application of alcohol to wounds might at times prove painful to patients, in no way do the physicians intend to maliciously inflict pain on their patients. Despite the pain experienced by patients, physicians recognize that certain treatment protocols are indispensable to the healing process.

Painful experiences provide us with opportunities to deepen our reliance on God because they arrest us and compel us to pay attention to what our heavenly Father is saying. Painful experiences demand that instead of surrendering to the adversity impacting our lives, we should assume a posture of stillness, waiting on directives from God that serve to transform our life situation. The prophet Isaiah reminds us of this truth: *"But they that **wait** upon the Lord shall renew their strength; they shall mount up with wings as eagles; they shall run, and not be weary; and they shall walk, and not faint"* (Isa. 40:31). Waiting on the Lord entails cultivating the spiritual insight to rely exclusively on the transformative action of God to radicalize our life situation as He fashions us into a home for Himself in this world, revealing that He has preeminence over any situation that might confront us on this side of glory.

Not only is faith numbered among the three theological virtues (see 1 Cor. 13:11), but it is also recognized as one of the seven fruits of the Spirit (see Gal. 5:22). And it is also the next rung on the ladder we are exhorted to grab hold of as we journey from the ravages of tribulation to a refuge of rest and restoration.

Reflection Questions

1. How has the exercise of faith during times of adversity, or the lack thereof, affected your spiritual formation?

2. What lifestyle changes, if any, might be effective in helping you to maximize the utilization of your faith?

3. Do you place a high premium on the deepening of your faith? What spiritual disciplines might be helpful to you in this endeavor?

CHAPTER FIVE

Exercise Patience in Difficult Times

The writer of Ecclesiastes informs us that there is a time for everything, and a season for every activity under the sun (see Eccles. 3:1). The words of the ancient scribe highlight the fact that every event in the universe has a duration or lifecycle of its own. As such, the manner by which we respond to events that threaten to degrade our sense of well-being ultimately affect the quality of the recovery process, because the way we respond to threatening circumstances will either help or hinder the process.

The apostle Paul is someone who was acquainted with the hardships of life, and he encourages modern-day pilgrims to exercise patience in those instances when we are confronted with adversity (see Rom. 12:12). Like Paul, the psalmist tells us that in those instances when we are assailed by adversity, we should wait on the Lord, allowing Him the opportunity to strengthen our heart (see Ps. 27:14). The inclination to exercise patience in those instances, however, when the gale forces of adversity buffet us is oftentimes the last piece of advice we are open to entertaining.

When adversity threatens to crack our lives open, we would prefer that the gale forces in whose surge we are immersed abate as quickly as possible, because human instinct for self-preservation influences us to engage in hasty retreats from storm situations.

Even though we might experience a sense of helplessness in those instances when we are assaulted by adversity, we are still able to mount effective responses that would enable us to survive the onslaught. As sailing ships adjust their sails to capture wind currents and navigate their way through the swell, we similarly possess the ability to employ strategies that could help us navigate our way through life's storms and survive the attending adversity.

Finding ourselves in thrall to stormy situations is often un-nerving to our sense of well-being because we are prone to feel like a tiny boat that is being tossed around on a turbulent sea, not always knowing which port we should turn to for help. But exercising patience affords the opportunity to center down and "catch our second wind," thereby engendering within us a semblance of calm that holds tensions in ways that enable us to better assess what is transpiring in our lives. Exercising patience grants us the opportunity to evaluate the attending adversity so we might devise effective responses to the besetting dilemma.

Patience: The Opportunity to Employ Constructive Responses to Difficult Situations

There is no way to be human without the experience of having one's heart broken. At some point on our pilgrimage through life, we will encounter difficulties so heartrending that we begin to question whether or not we really want to continue living. It is the human tendency to respond to difficult situations by doing whatever is necessary to eliminate the pain that is impacting our existence. But instead of always employing the most effective responses, we at times shut down emotionally, turn toward anger and bitterness, ingest drugs, and unfortunately even adopt a cynical outlook on life. We employ various coping strategies with the expectation that they will help us address difficult situations in constructive ways. But many of the strategies we employ merely tend to exacerbate the predicament in which we find ourselves. So, instead of being our salvation, they propel us into negative states where we languish for extensive periods of time. Patience is a powerful medicine in such instances because it has the potential to transform a wounded, shutdown heart as we remain open and receptive to transformative insights that could offer us new life.

Patience changes the rhythm of life by encouraging us to think critically about our predicament before rushing into action. As such, we are prevented from employing counterproductive responses to our pain-predicament or hiding out in states of negativity where our heart remains an unhealed wound that we keep entombed within us for a long time. Instead of reacting impulsively to adversity and setting ourselves up to being overwhelmed by the difficulties impacting our lives, patience gives us the opportunity to be still and wait prayerfully on the power of God to arrest us, providing us insight that ultimately brings effective responses to our conscious awareness which resolves our problem situation.

Patience additionally affords us the opportunity to *rest* in God's love and complete dependence, thereby availing us to sustenance from the source of healing and renewal that is able to mend our brokenness into a healed and unified whole. Further still, patience enables us to keep God at the center of our awareness. And by so doing, live each day with a sense of expectancy that the life of God will work through us to effectuate the transformation of our life situation.

Patience: Acknowledging and Naming Our Suffering Honestly and Openly

Difficult experiences oftentimes traumatize us to our very core, shocking our sense of well-being. Because the pain that comes in tow with difficult experiences is many times so overwhelming, it threatens to unravel us to the core or throw us into states of disequilibrium. However, when we choose to practice patience, we are able to maintain the requisite poise that enables us to name and claim our suffering. The practice of patience enables us to acknowledge our vulnerability and to deal openly and honestly with our suffering instead of driving the suffering soul back into hiding.

An illuminating African proverb states: "He who hides his disease cannot be healed." This proverbial statement lends credence to the truth that we will never experience healing in those areas of our lives which we refuse to acknowledge as being sick. By acknowledging our vulnerability, we can become intimately acquainted with the forces that threaten to degrade our sense of well-being. And by so doing, we can take the necessary steps to address the affected areas of our lives. This is extremely important because being able to identify the forces that threaten to degrade our sense of well-being is indispensable to the recovery process. We must be able to diagnose what is making us sick before we can apply the prescription that is needed to cure the attending sickness. Diagnosis always precedes prescription.

After identifying the forces that are afflicting us, it is highly recommended that we solicit therapeutic and spiritual help to assist us in the resolution of our dilemma. Therapeutic intervention provides us with strategies that enable us to work through difficult situations, while spiritual help affords us the opportunity to avail ourselves to divine therapy. Spiritual help also gives us the opportunity to reflect on how our life story is linked to God's unfolding story, which also enables us to gain a deeper perspective as to how we are availing ourselves to God. Spiritual help also provides us with insights that enable us to better align our lives with God's plan to bring about transformation in our life situation.

Dr. Edward P. Wimberly is one of America's most distinguished scholars and writers in the area of pastoral care. He is a Professor of Pastoral Care at Interdenominational Theological Seminary in Atlanta. Dr. Wimberley recognizes the importance of linking our individual life story with God's unfolding story in those instances when adversity assails us so that we might experience transformation of our life situation.

Writing in *African American Pastoral Care*, Dr. Wimberly indicates that African-American pastors skillfully employ the use of biblical narratives to address the normal crises with which parishioners are confronted on a daily basis, helping them capture a glimpse of hope in the midst of suffering. He references the work of Henry Mitchell and Nicholas Lewter in *Soul Theology*,[1] where the authors refer to the employment of biblical narratives as soul theology—the core belief system that gives shape to the world in a meaningful way. Mitchell and Lewter believe that by drawing on the biblical narrative reservoir when ministering to parishioners, African-American pastors are able to suggest ways that motivate people to action, help them see themselves in a new light, help them recognize new resources, enable them to channel behaviors in constructive ways, bring healing and reconciliation in relationships, heal the scars of memories, and provide guidance when direction is needed.[2]

In Dr. Wimberley's estimation, the application of biblical narratives to the life situation of African-American Christians is an effective therapeutic tool because it enables them to view their life situation through the lens of biblical narratives. As people who have been subjected to oppression and marginalization from the mainstream of American society, not only are African-American Christians able to see God's purpose in and for the world revealed through the teachings of the Bible, they are also able to identify with a Savior, whom, like they, experienced oppression and marginalization during His life on earth. As such, they are able to recognize Him as the exemplar and guarantor of God's redemptive love. This truth supports Paul's premise that Jesus is a High Priest who is acquainted with every facet of our life situation (see Heb. 2:17).

Because African-American Christians recognize through biblical narratives that God is actively working on their behalf to resolve life's pressing problems, they are able to entrust their circumstances to the Creator in the memory of the crucified One who sits exalted at the right hand of the Father in heaven interceding on their behalf. Armed with this liberating insight, African-American Christians are able to avail themselves to God's providential care and open the corridors of their spirit to the consoling power of God's divine energies.

Patience: Journeying to the Heart of Difficult Situations

After naming and claiming our suffering, the practice of patience creates in us the opportunity to move directly to the heart of the besetting dilemma. It enables us to confront our pain-predicament in its full magnitude instead of numbing our bodies with anesthetics, which our pain-avoiding culture teaches us to do in the attempt to "take the edge off" and better cope with life. Exercising patience opens us up to receiving insights from God that could be employed to address the thorny issues of life. It enables us to recognize that difficulties must be faced rather than feared. It additionally enables us to recognize that confronting our pain-predicament reduces the intensity of the experience because confrontation provides us with a freeing effect that prevents pain from spiritually and emotionally dominating and crippling us. When we seek to identify the root cause of the pain-generating forces impacting our existence, the tension ensuing from the sense of helplessness we experience in those instances when we attempt to avoid pain is reduced and eliminated.

Exercising patience affords us the opportunity to become attentive to our pain-predicament, assuming responsibility for what is transpiring in our lives instead of fleeing the scene with distractions or attacking and blaming external sources. It enables us to "be still," and recognize that every event in life is a teachable moment. Exercising patience also enables us to recognize that problems never go away when they are ignored. And that they need to be acknowledged, addressed, and worked through because, if this course of action is not pursued, problems will fester and remain an impediment to our growth and well-being. Further still, exercising patience enables us to recognize that life under any condition is worth fighting for. And that it is never too late to fix those aspects of our lives that are broken so we might live in a more meaningful and productive way. Armed with this mindset, we are able to view difficulties as opportunities to transform adversity into experiences that ultimately prove to be life-enlarging instead of life-diminishing.

Nineteenth-century Danish philosopher Soren Kierkegaard wrote in *The Sickness Unto Death* about the dyads that populate the self. He indicated that each dyad has a side that is expansive, and one that is limiting.[3] Adversity in any of its varied guises is a dyad that could shrink or enlarge our ability to access abundant life. It could render us less creative when we choose to surrender to forces that threaten to degrade our sense of well-being, thereby influencing us to give up on life. On the other hand, it could also enlarge us because it presents us with the opportunity to drill deep into the source that is life-enhancing and life-enlarging, and discover ways to live more abundantly. When we purpose in our heart to never surrender to negative forces, we manifest the mindset described by Paul Tillich as "the courage to be."[4] By purposing to become more emboldened in our spirit, we cultivate the determination of never surrendering to the forces of negativity because we recognize that acquiescence is fatal to our sense of well-being.

By employing expository writing as a means of throwing the spotlight on his turbulent life experiences, Russian novelist Alexander Solzhenitsyn brought the world's attention to the once secretive and inhumane Gulag—the Soviet Union's forced labor camp system. In 1945, Solzhenitsyn was incarcerated in a series of camps in the Soviet's notorious prison system, nestled deep in the desolate and inhospitable regions of Siberia by the communist megalomaniac, Joseph Stalin. Stalin incarcerated him because of his diatribes against the policies of the communist regime. During his period of incarceration, he experienced a conversion to the Christian faith. After being released from prison in 1953, he was exiled to the Soviet republic of Kazakhstan. Writing about his experiences in *The Gulag Archipelago*, the dissident indicated:

It was only when I lay there on the rotting straw that I sensed within myself the first stirrings of good. Gradually it was disclosed to me that the line separating good and evil passes not through states, nor between classes, nor between political parties either—but right through every human heart.... I nourished my soul there, and I say without hesitation: Bless you prison for saving my life.[5]

Unlike scores of his suffering brethren who surrendered their fate to the inhumane conditions of the oppressive Gulag, Solzhenitsyn struggled with every atom of willpower to prevent himself from falling prey to the difficulties impacting his life situation, thereby enabling him to respond in a manner that was life-expanding rather than life-diminishing. He recognized that ultimately life still had meaning, despite the fact that he had been stripped of every last vestige of human freedom. However, by choosing to exercise patience and respond to his pain-predicament in the manner that he did, the 1970 Nobel Laureate in literature drew sustenance from the reservoir of resiliency welling up at the core of his being, thereby enabling him to survive the adversity impacting his existence in the confines of the wretched universe.

Patience: The Opportunity to Employ Tools That Effectively Manage Anger

History teaches us that when people hurt, they are prone to become angry. Anger is a normal response to the experience of being hurt. Not only does anger sap our energy and drain us of vital energy that could be utilized to seek a closer walk with God, it also degrades our health and well-being. However, while anger might ensue from hurt feelings or some other inner turbulence, it is not in and of itself sinful. But if it is left unaddressed, unresolved anger could influence us to engage in patterns of behavior that are unhealthy and displeasing to God.

Scripture tells us that when we are subjected to feelings of anger, we should not allow it to dominate and propel us into patterns of sinful behavior (see Ps. 4:4). As moral agents, we possess the personal power to prevent anger from escalating to the point where it causes us to engage in patterns of behavior that are destructive to our well-being. Even though anger might on occasion prove to be overwhelming, we ultimately possess the agency to take charge, direct, and control our responses to such feelings. It is imperative that we gain insight as to how we might arm ourselves with proactive measures that prevent us from becoming consumed by feelings of anger and indulge in patterns of behavior that are detrimental to our sense of well-being, and thus displeasing to God. In like manner, as Jesus drew on examples from nature to unpack His life-enlarging principles to His disciples, it might also be helpful for us to draw on nature to obtain greater clarity as to how anger impacts our well-being. We might take our cues from weather phenomena.

When different types of atmospheric elements interact with each other, they undergo chemical reactions that result in the formation of completely new substances. The new substances result in the formation of weather cells or areas in the atmosphere containing high amounts of electrical energy. These high-energy areas occasionally produce states of instability or disequilibrium in the atmosphere. While individual weather cells produce states of disequilibrium over limited geographical areas, multiple cells combine to form weather systems containing high concentrations of electrical energy which at times extend over large geographical areas. Meteorologists refer to the extended areas as "weather fronts."

Nature always strives to attain a semblance of stability or equilibrium, and in scientific terminology this is referred to as *entropy*. Unstable atmospheric cells achieve equilibrium or *entropy* by unloading high levels of electrical energy that they are carrying into the surrounding atmosphere, which is the genesis of rainstorms, snowstorms, windstorms, tornadoes, and all of the adverse weather phenomena with which we are quite familiar. After unstable cells unburden themselves of high levels of electrical energy they are carrying, a state of equilibrium is attained. And weather conditions revert to a semblance of normalcy that is referred to in the parlance of everyday language as "the calm after the storm."

In those instances when we hurt or become subjected to inner turbulence, we experience increased levels of tension in our bodies if the underlying feelings are not adequately resolved. Increased tension levels result in increased levels of adrenaline being released into the bloodstream in the effort to help us cope with the destabilizing effects of the increased tension. Adrenaline is nature's hormone that enables us to respond to life-threatening situations. However, levels of adrenaline above the amounts normally found in the bloodstream serve as fuel that bring about adverse physiological changes in our bodies, such as increased contraction of certain types of muscles, increased heart rates, increased pulse rates, and increased respiratory rates. Abnormal levels of adrenaline in the bloodstream also cloud our ability to think constructively on account of our altered physiology.

So when anger is not adequately resolved in its early stages and allowed to escalate to the point where we lose mastery over ourselves, physiologically speaking we are in a state of disequilibrium. Similar to unstable weather cells discharging high levels of electrical energy into the atmosphere, humans at times unconsciously engage in actions that are designed to discharge high levels of tension from our bodies in order to achieve a semblance of equilibrium—to calm us down. This activity is referred to in scientific terms as *catharsis*. And it is attained by screaming, crying, hitting, throwing temper tantrums, or indulging in other unhealthy responses. However, cathartic measures might also be achieved in ways that are constructive.

In far too many instances, angry people do not know what to do with their feelings of anger. As a result, they engage in unhealthy responses by lashing out at other people or things. Without understanding why they lash out at things or other people, they unknowingly engage in cathartic measures that are intended to unload the high levels of tension that are coursing through their bodies, expecting to attain an appearance of calm within themselves. Unfortunately, unhealthy attempts to unload tension which has not been carefully thought out invariably results in physical damage to things, and at times hurt to oneself and other people. Further still, unhealthy responses to unload tension oftentimes result in death of self and others. It is important that we gain insight as to how we might engage in proactive measures to address feelings of anger in ways that produce desirable outcomes instead of affording anger the opportunity to exert control over us, causing us to engage in unhealthy patterns of behavior.

After recognizing that we are subjected to feelings of anger, the first thing we should do to prevent our feelings from dominating us is to relinquish them to the authority of God. The Bible exhorts us to cast our cares and anxieties on the Lord because He cares for us (see 1 Pet. 5:7). In certain theological circles, this mindset is referred to as "offering up" our circumstances to God. In very much the same way that Jesus commanded tempestuous weather conditions on the Sea of Galilee to be still (see Matt. 8:23; Mark 4:35-39; Luke 8:22-24), we might likewise entrust feelings of anger to the authority of God so that we might receive divine assistance that enables us to retain mastery over our emotions.

However, while we might not be able to instinctively turn our emotions on and off in the same manner that we turn water on and off in a faucet, we must remain vigilant about keeping feelings of anger under subjection to the authority of God. In those instances when we relinquish feelings of anger to the authority of God, we give up dependence on our ability to battle the forces that are creating turbulence within us. By giving up the human struggle to battle against the forces creating turbulence within our spirit, the Holy Spirit works with our spirit to bring about a semblance of calm within us, thereby enabling us to retain mastery over our emotions. The Holy Spirit has the supernatural ability to provide us with insight that will enable us to adequately address any besetting dilemma. While we might not understand how God's power works within us to regulate the physiology of our bodies, we must recognize that He created us and He knows how to make us whole. David reminds us of this truth when he indicated that we are fearfully and wonderfully made (see Ps. 139:14).

There are instances in life when disturbing events cause feelings of anger to erupt within us that are oftentimes referred to as "righteous indignation," such as the mindless and random killing of innocent bystanders in drive-by shootings, robbery, rape, and other tragic acts of violence that are visited on the person of innocent individuals. In such instances, we do have the right to own our feelings because we should be upset by the outcomes generated by destructive forces that plague our communities. But we must also remember to "offer up" feelings of indignation to God so that He might give us insight that helps us retain mastery over ourselves and prevents us from acting in ways that are displeasing to Him. Additionally, we must recognize that feelings of "righteous indignation" might be God's way of prompting us to become involved in working to eliminate the pervasiveness of life-diminishing forces that impact our communities and, by so doing, bear the light of Christ into the darkness of our time.

In addition to volitionally "offering up" feelings of anger to God through the practice of prayer, we might also engage in physical exercise to decrease high levels of tension that accompany sensations of anger within our bodies. The Bible tells us that physical exercise is beneficial to our sense of well-being. It helps us keep feelings of anger under control because it breaks us away from our normal routine and affords us the opportunity to relax and reflect on what is transpiring in our lives. By so doing, we are better able to respond to problems in a constructive manner.

Physical exercise is also a release valve for tensions because it burns up adrenaline in the bloodstream that fuel tensions. By burning up excess amounts of adrenaline above the amounts normally found in the bloodstream, tension levels are reduced. In addition to helping reduce high levels of tension, physical exercise also helps our bodies eliminate waste products through sweat, which has a positive effect on our general health and well-being. This is because if toxic substances which are generated by the body's metabolic activities are not eliminated in a timely manner, they reach unhealthy levels and poison our systems. Illnesses resulting from the unhealthy buildup of toxic substances subject us to unwarranted stress. This means that sweating is a useful means of eliminating unhealthy wastes from our bodies.

Physical exercise also serves to promote healthy muscle tone and cardiovascular health, both of which are proven stress reducers. Further still, it has a regulatory effect on interdependent physiological systems, thereby enabling them to function within normal limits, and engendering a semblance of equilibrium that is referred to in medical terminology as *homeostasis*.

In addition to the above-mentioned benefits accruing from physical exercise, medical science has also concluded that during periods of physical exercise, the human brain releases chemicals known as endorphins into the bloodstream. Endorphins create sensations that are referred to in the parlance of exercise physiology as the "runner's high," and in medical parlance as "feel-good" hormones. Scientists are of the opinion that endorphins provide a boost to our immune system, in addition to producing sensations of overall well-being, both of which enable us to cultivate a positive outlook on life. They also act as counterbalances to self-destructive emotions, preventing us from becoming overwhelmed by feelings of anger and acting in ways that are self-destructive and displeasing to God.

Another effective technique for dealing with feelings of anger is to engage in breathing exercises, commonly referred to as "controlled breathing." We accomplish this feat by assuming a comfortable sitting position, closing our eyes, and concentrating on our thoughts. After assuming a comfortable posture, we breathe deeply through the diaphragm, the dome-shaped muscular sheet that is attached to the lower ribs, dividing the chest cavity from the stomach. By engaging in breathing exercises, we are able to engender a semblance of calm within our bodies that enables us to explore the root cause of feelings of anger, thereby enabling us to respond to the disturbing feelings in constructive ways, helping us retain mastery over ourselves.

Medical research has concluded that controlled breathing has a regulatory effect on centers in the brain that affect the heart and respiratory systems. Additionally, controlled breathing enables our blood to become saturated with adequate amounts of oxygen. Adequate amounts of oxygen uptake prevents us from hyperventilating and placing additional stress on the heart, as is the case when we become excited during fits of anger and fail to take deep breaths that fill our lungs with needed oxygen. When the bloodstream is saturated with adequate amounts of oxygen, the heart is able to function within normal limits because it does not have to work extra hard to pump additional volumes of blood to oxygen-deprived tissues. However, when there is an insufficient uptake of oxygen, as in the case of shallow breathing, the heart muscle is compelled to work extra hard to furnish body tissues with adequate amounts of oxygen. The struggle to pump additional volumes of oxygen-rich blood to oxygen-deprived tissues places additional stress on the heart muscle.

Controlled breathing can also be combined with visualization, where we imagine the oxygen that we're inhaling as God's breath—*rûah*—washing and cleansing our blood and body tissues of sensations of anger and other impurities. Embracing the belief that the breath of God coursing through our bodies has the ability to render us free from anger and other impurities engenders a semblance of calm within us and prevents us from acting in ways that are self-destructive and displeasing to God.

Yet another effective technique that could be employed to prevent anger from escalating to the point where we engage in activities that are unhealthy and displeasing to God is meditation. Even though meditation is not as popular in the West or Occident, and is predominantly an Eastern or Oriental tradition, it affords us the opportunity to break away from our normal routine, look into ourselves, and touch what is transpiring within the deep recesses of our being. By assuming a comfortable sitting position and practicing controlled breathing techniques, and by allowing our emotions to float to the surface of our consciousness, we are then able to discern dominant emotions and gain insight as to why we are feeling the way we do. By looking deep into ourselves, we are able to address problem situations instead of reacting impulsively to our feelings and fail to employ carefully-thought-out strategies that are helpful in resolving the attending adversity.

Meditation can be combined with controlled breathing, and it can also be combined with select verses of Scripture, positive affirmations, or silently repeating the *Jesus Prayer*: "Lord Jesus Christ, Son of God, have mercy upon me, a sinner." The first half of the prayer could be repeated while inhaling deeply through the nostrils, and the second half could be repeated while exhaling slowly through the mouth. For example, during inhalation the practitioner would repeat, "Lord Jesus Christ, Son of God," and while exhaling they would repeat, "Have mercy upon me, a sinner." By engaging in this exercise, not only are we able to look deep into ourselves in order to ascertain the root cause of feelings of discomfort, we are also able to petition God's help in resolving any besetting dilemma.

Employing any item on the suggested menu of exercises could be effective in helping us attain mastery over ourselves in those instances when we are subjected to feelings of anger. They are beneficial in two distinct ways: First, they afford us the opportunity to employ volitional measures that serve to bring feelings of anger under our control. And secondly, as time progresses during which we are engaged in the exercises, high levels of adrenaline in the bloodstream attain normal levels. When levels of adrenaline attain clinical parameters, tension levels decrease because the high levels of adrenaline that sustain tension are reduced. As a result of reduced levels of tension, sensations of anger are reduced. And the likelihood of us engaging in behaviors that are counterproductive and displeasing to God are eventually reduced and eliminated.

Patience: The Opportunity to Grieve Our Pain-Predicament

We live in a culture that is overly preoccupied with speed and displays high levels of intolerance and indifference toward the issue of suffering. In an attempt to hide their suffering, individuals who are subjected to painful situations are oftentimes influenced to ignore, deny, and suppress the pain that is impacting their being. Instead of allowing themselves adequate time to grieve their pain-predicament, they tend to rush past the experience in an attempt to resume a normal lifestyle. Because they attempt to get back into their regular routine before adequately addressing what is ailing them, they remain impaired. And remaining impaired tends to hobble their abilities and prevent them from functioning in an effective manner, thus exacerbating the predicament.

In those instances when we are subjected to trauma that ensues from some pain-predicament, it is important to refrain from ignoring the attending pain or engaging in activities that are designed to make us feel artificially upbeat. It is important to allow the grieving process to run its course. Feeling sad is a natural response to being hurt, and each individual recovers from trauma at his or her own pace. In like manner, as our physical bodies require adequate time to heal, the human spirit also requires adequate time to mend in those instances when trauma ensuing from adversity has impacted it. There is no set timetable on the healing process, and everyone heals at his or her own pace. Therefore, it is imperative that we acknowledge those instances when we are hurt, allowing the healing process to evolve according to its own natural rhythm so that we might regain a semblance of wholeness.

Patience: Cultivating a Spirit of Compassion

In addition to living in a fast-paced culture, we also live in a culture that demonstrates high levels of intolerance toward human frailty. In a celebrity-addicted culture that is overly obsessed with pandering to superheroes, suffering people frequently find themselves minimized and marginalized from the mainstream of society and compelled to live in the shadows as "invisible citizens" intent on concealing their vulnerability. However, a serious bout with adversity has the potential of bringing us face-to-face with our inherent vulnerability in ways that serve to render us more compassionate and magnanimous toward the plight of our suffering brethren. Cultivating the spirit of compassion helps us recognize the reality of our shared humanity. It also has the potential of transforming us into "wounded healers," as Roman Catholic priest and spiritual writer Henri Nouwen taught us to say.[6] Difficult experiences have the potential of enlarging our capacity for empathy—the *pathos* by which we cultivate the capacity to bring ourselves in solidarity with the suffering of others, thereby giving relevancy to the oft-repeated slogan: "There, but for the grace of God, go I."

Compassion means to "suffer with" our brothers and sisters. It enables us to see ourselves as inextricably linked to the universal human family and recognize that in the grand scheme of things we are our brothers' and sisters' brother and sister. This interrelated structure of reality is chronicled in *Strength to Love*, by Martin Luther King Jr., when he declared: "All men are caught up in an inescapable network of mutuality, tied in a single garment of destiny. Whatever affects one directly affects all indirectly. I can never be what I ought to be until you are what you ought to be, and you can never be what you ought to be until I am what I ought to be."[7] The sentiments of the civil rights icon resonate with those of the ancient Greek mystic Plotinus, who purportedly wrote someplace: "If we are in unity with the Spirit, we are in unity with each other, and so we are all one." Plotinus's insightful sentiment points to the underlying interconnectedness of all life, highlighting the imperative for each soul to engage in intentional *koinonia*—the fellowship that enables us to radicalize our perspective on life in ways that engender compassion toward our fellow human beings. Compassion reminds us of the African idiom: "A person is a person through other persons."

Since each human being is a vital link in the chain of God's family, and we belong to each other, it is imperative that we engage in collaborative efforts that will help inaugurate what Dr. King envisioned as "The Beloved Community." It is also beneficial when we co-labor with our heavenly Father to cultivate the requisite level of patience, whereby we are equipped to engage in efforts that enable us to embrace the divine mandate of loving our neighbor as we love ourselves. *It is imperative that we love our neighbors as we love ourselves because the survival of the local and global community is contingent on our ability to love our neighbor as we love ourselves. God loves our neighbors, and He paid the ultimate price by sacrificing His only begotten Son on a cruel Roman cross for them.* Calvary is the signature act of God and demonstrates the depth to which He stoops in order to redeem a fallen people back to Himself.

Like faith and patience, love is numbered among the three theological virtues (see 1 Cor. 13:11) and is recognized as one of the seven fruits of the Spirit (see Gal. 5:22). Love is the next rung of the ladder we are exhorted to grab hold of as we journey from a place of hurt to a place of healing.

Reflection Questions

1. How has the practice of patience, or the lack thereof, impacted your ability to adequately cope with difficult circumstances?

2. What are some things you might do that will help you increase your practice of patience?

3. In what ways might the practice of patience improve your individual overall well-being, the well-being of your local community, and the world at large?

CHAPTER SIX

Keep Love Alive in Difficult Times

M. Scott Peck, M.D., indicates that in our attempts to examine the issue of love, we are merely toying with mystery. The distinguished author and physician is of the opinion that love is too large and too deep an issue to be truly understood or measured within the limited framework of words.[1] Even though love's description is beyond the reach of customary narrative frames, it is the single most necessary component in human life. And it is indisputably the very heartbeat of human existence, because God is love (see 1 John 4:8). Saint Augustine believes that God is known and experienced most in the act of love, of which He is the source.[2] David G. Benner provides us with another insightful perspective, indicating: "God is love's origin. But so too is God's end. Love given to others in need is love given to God. Love is always God flowing through us and back again to God."[3]

We must be extremely careful not to confuse love with a mere sentimental outpouring or sense of ecstasy that we experience in the human body. Love is an intangible commodity, and something much deeper than the sensations we could ever experience by way of the objective senses. Because of this, no one has ever fully arrived at a truly satisfactory definition of love. However, by employing words borrowed from the Greek language, we are better able to shed much-needed illumination on the elusive subject.

The Greek language employs four words in its attempt to describe various types of love. The first word is *eros* (pronounced *air-ohs*), which is the root of the word *erotic*. It is a sort of aesthetic or romantic love that is characterized by intense emotional attachment and powerful sexual feelings or desires. In the Platonic dialogues, *eros* is the soul's yearning to approximate the realm of the divine. The second word is *philia* (pronounced *feel-e-ah*), a reciprocal love and intimate affection between friends. *Storge* (pronounced *stor-gay*), is the third type of love, describing familial affection of parents for children, and siblings for each other, as well as the love between cousins. However, *storge* is not limited to families, or even to humans, because it is the kind of affection capable of developing between college roommates, military service-members, co-workers, and between individuals and their pets.

The fourth word is *agape* (pronounced *ah-gah-pay*), which means "love feast." *Agape* emphasizes unselfish concerns for the beloved's needs, even when that requires personal sacrifice. Often referred to as altruistic love, *agape* is the creative redemptive goodwill for all men whereby we love our fellow human beings, not just because we like them or because their ways appeal to us. We love them because they are created in the image and likeness of God, and because God loves them. Belgian priest Louis Everly suggests that in order to be the sons and daughters of God, we must first be brothers and sisters to God's other children.[4] In the final analysis, *agape* means loving our fellow human beings without expecting anything in return—loving them without having an agenda.

At the very heart of the Christian message is God's love for His creation. The apostle John writes: *"Herein is love, not that we loved God, but that He **loved** us, and sent His Son to be the propitiation for our sins"* (1 John 4:10). The sacrificial death of Jesus on Calvary's Cross is the eternal expression of God's love descending from heaven to earth to redeem a fallen people back from the slave market of sin. Calvary is the sublime expression of God's *agape* for humanity because He was willing to sacrifice His only joy in order to reestablish the human family in a right relationship with Him and, by so doing, breach the rift that ensued from Adam and Eve's rebellion in the Garden of Eden. God sent His Son to help—to make the world right again (see John 3:16-17).

While no one would ever be able to fully plumb the inexhaustible depths of God's ability to love His creation, down through the centuries several individuals have purposed in their heart to live out Jesus's admonition of loving their neighbor as they love themselves. The life of the late Mother Teresa of Calcutta bespeaks the essence of a noble and gentle woman who made every possible attempt to love her neighbor as she loved herself.

Mother Teresa was an Albanian nun, who at age 16 took her final vows into the Loreto Order, an Irish community of nuns with missions to India, on May 24, 1937, exchanging the name Gonda for Teresa. During a retreat on September 19, 1946, while travelling in India by train, she had a conversion to "the poorest of the poor." Throughout her travels, she observed human tragedies lining the streets of overcrowded cities where scores of destitute Indians lay suffering and dying without the least trace of human dignity. Her observations touched her at the very core of her being, influencing her to establish the Missionaries of Charity in Calcutta. She received permission from the city government to utilize an old Kali temple as her base of operations. And in lieu of a nun's habit, she and her sympathizers wore traditional saris, the principal outer garment of Hindu women, undertaking efforts to help the dying depart this earthly plane of existence with a sense of dignity. They tenderly and compassionately washed the faces of the dying souls with cool refreshing water and were always present at the event of their passing in order to ensure that the dying souls departed this earthly plane with the acknowledgement that someone cared about their welfare.

There were cynics in the local community who entertained suspicions that Mother Teresa had ulterior motives. They believed she merely employed her missionary endeavors as a way to convert Indians to the Christian religion, even though she and her co-workers did not evangelize nor minister to the poor in the name of Christ. This belief prompted several disgruntled members of the community to launch a brazen attack on the old temple, hurling stones at the mission. During the assault on the edifice, windows were shattered, and flying shards of broken glass inflicted gaping wounds on the bodies of several women inside. Despite the assault on Mother Teresa's headquarters, she and her associates refused to abandon their ministrations to the suffering masses that were entrusted to their care and continued catering to the needs of the dying, gently wiping their faces with moist towels and providing them with fluids to drink during their final moments on this side of glory.

When the attackers, consisting of Hindus, atheists, and communists, observed that there was no response from inside the temple, they became curious and were determined to find out what was transpiring behind the temple walls. The predators barged into the mission armed with stones and clubs, eyes ablaze with anger. When the mob arrived inside the temple, they were moved by the unshaken will of Mother Teresa and her co-workers as they ministered to the needs of those dying with a deep sense of serenity. Touched by what he observed, the ringleader dropped his clubs and declared to Mother Teresa, "I do not believe in the God you believe, nor the Christianity you brought into, but I believe in what you are doing." The contrite convert abandoned his aggressive behavior and proceeded to assist Mother Teresa and her colleagues in cleaning up the mess that he and his followers created during the attack on the old temple. After the incident, the attackers remained ardent supporters of the compassionate nun from Albania, in her efforts to serve the poor and downtrodden of Calcutta.[5]

At the end of her life, Mother Teresa's Missionaries of Charity, which was started with only the clothes on her back and five Indian rupees (an amount of money than is less than one U.S. dollar), were active in 77 countries, with 350 communities involving thousands of sisters. In 1997, at the advanced age of 87, a Nobel Peace Prize solidified her worldwide acclaim, thereby showcasing her contribution to humanity. In describing her life in an interview before her death, Mother Teresa purportedly stated: "I am a pencil in the hand of a writing God, who is sending a love letter to the world."

In 1994 the world became appalled over the brutal genocide that transpired in the East Central African nation of Rwanda, where over 800,000 people of the Tutsi tribe were systematically exterminated by rampaging hordes of their Hutu countrymen.

The historical dramatic film *Hotel Rwanda* chronicles the heroic exploits of Paul Rusesabgina, courageous hotelier of the Hotel des Mille Collines, in Rwanda's capital city of Kigali. Rusesabgina utilized his political position, social skills, and quick wit to rescue over 1,200 mostly Tutsis who sought sanctuary within the protective walls of the now world-famous Dutch-owned hotel. Even though his life was threatened by murderous gangs of Hutu militiamen who laid siege to his establishment for several weeks, Rusesabgina could very well have chosen to act in his enlightened self-interest to save his life and those of his family by allowing murderers that were hell bent on exterminating the lives of their Tutsi fellow citizens to enter the hotel and continue the pogrom that was taking place in the surrounding community. However, by summoning the best angels within his nature, the hotelier refused to cooperate with his fellow tribesmen, availing himself instead to be used as an instrument of the holy, dispensing mercy to those who were being oppressed, despite the fact that they were not members of his ethnic community. The lives of Tutsis seeking refuge in Rusesabgina's hotel were eventually saved because of the selfless actions of the courageous and compassionate hotelier.

On account of their unselfish actions where both individuals placed the self-interest of their fellow human beings before their own, Mother Teresa and Paul Rusesabgina demonstrated God's *agape* in a form described by Quaker theologian Jeremy Taylor as "*amor mundi*"—love for the entire world. Taylor describes *amor mundi* as the kind of love where God hurls the world into our hearts, where we and He together carry it in infinitely tender love.[6] Simone Weil states, "In denying oneself, one becomes capable under God of establishing someone else by creative affirmation. One gives oneself in ransom for the other. It is a redemptive act."[7] Mother Teresa's and Paul Rusesabgina's love ethic is proof positive that love is not restricted to any particular ethnic group. Instead, it is a life force ensuing from Almighty God that is dispensed across all ethnic lines.

The actions of Mother Teresa and Paul Rusesabgina additionally highlight the fact that even though someone might not be directly engaged in the act of oppressing their neighbor, they are still saddled with the awesome responsibility of addressing injustice in any of its existent forms. Wayne Muller indicates, "It quickly becomes impossible to accuse any one person [or group] of evil, because we constantly hide behind a society afflicted with injustice that acts as our surrogate, and enfolds us all in an insidious complicity in institutional harm done quietly, invisibly, carelessly."[8] Mother Teresa and Paul Rusesabgina recognized the imperative of becoming tributaries of God's *agape*, and both acted in ways that served to enrich humanity. The actions of the two individuals remind us that love oftentimes has a very high premium attached to it.

Just as Jesus sacrificed His life for humankind, engaging in acts of love does on occasion cost people their lives. However, despite the high premium attached to love, God desires that we cultivate the moral imagination that would engender positive changes in our local and global communities. This becomes possible when we abandon ourselves to the Holy Spirit so that we might be utilized as conduits of grace, making God's promised "new thing" a reality on earth. By incarnating God's love at the core of our being, we become equipped to shed much-needed light into the darkened areas of our world.

An inspiring story that highlights the occasion where someone crossed the ethnic divide and exposed himself to potential danger is the parable of the Good Samaritan (see Luke 10:30-37). The New Testament report chronicles the harrowing experiences of a wayfarer who was travelling from Jerusalem to Jericho. At some point along the 17-mile journey, brazen thugs set upon him, beating and robbing him of his valuables and clothing. After assaulting the victim, the attackers fled the scene, leaving him battered and half dead on the side of the dangerous roadway. Shortly after the brutal attack, a priest was travelling the same route. Unfortunately, when he observed the victim languishing on the roadway, he crossed over to the other side, throwing nervous glances over his shoulders as he hastily departed the scene. Shortly after the priest had passed by, a Levite also came along. In like manner, the Levite crossed over to the other side of the roadway when he observed the body of the victim lying on the side of the thoroughfare. And like the priest before him, he proceeded on his way without stopping to render assistance to the suffering soul.

After the two religious clerics had departed the scene, a Samaritan came along. Unlike the priest and Levite before him, when he noticed the victim lying on the side of the road, he had compassion on him. The Samaritan dismounted his beast, hurried to the location where the victim lay, and began pouring oil and wine into his wounds, bandaging them up. He then placed the wounded wayfarer onto his beast of burden and transported him to a nearby inn, where he cared for him throughout the night. Before departing on his business ventures the following morning, the Samaritan left a monetary deposit of two denarii (approximately 40 cents of modern currency) with the innkeeper, instructing him to continue caring for the convalescing patient. He further informed the proprietor that if the cost of caring for the man were to exceed the amount of money that was left on deposit, he would reimburse him for any additional expenses that were incurred on his return trip to the inn.

There is no concrete evidence provided in Luke's report as to why neither the priest nor the Levite stopped to render first aid to their suffering brother. However, the Reverend Dr. Martin Luther King Jr. posited several reasons that might have influenced their reluctance to stop. First, when the religious clerics encountered the wounded man on the side of the road, neither could delay their arrival at an important religious meeting to which they were headed at the time. Secondly, they were intimately aware of the fact that Jewish religious law prohibited them from touching the corpse of a stranger, since any such action on their part would render them ritually impure (see Lev. 21:1-4). Dr. King suggested that in all likelihood, both the priest and Levite assumed that the man was already dead when they encountered him on the side of the road, instead of merely being unconscious. Because of this assumption, they were reluctant to establish contact with the supposedly dead body. Further still, Dr. King jokingly assumed that both men might have been on their way to an organizational meeting of the Jericho Road Improvement Association. Whatever the real reason might have been that prevented them from stopping, neither individual took the initiative to render life-saving medical assistance to their brother in his time of need.[9]

While Dr. King did employ some levity in surmising why neither the priest nor the Levite stopped to render medical assistance to the wounded wayfarer, he did provide several valid reasons in addition to the previously mentioned prohibitions as to why the two individuals might have acted the way they did. The first reason being, they were simply afraid to stop. During ancient

times the Jericho road was recognized as a dangerous thoroughfare that was infested with ruthless highway brigands, and was
infamously referred to in the parlance of the street as the "bloody
pass." It reality, Jericho Road was nothing more than a narrow
footpath winding its way along the edge of a rugged and treacherous mountain range. Jerusalem stands at an elevation of 2,000
feet above sea level, while Jericho stands at an elevation of 1,000
feet below sea level. The precipitous descent from Jerusalem
to Jericho is a distance less than 20 miles along a meandering
mountain road that is populated with sudden hairpin turns, and
desolate caves that afford plenty of opportune hiding places for
would-be ambushers to launch preemptive attacks against unsuspecting travelers.

Well aware of the notoriety of the crime-infested roadway,
both men might have entertained suspicions that the highway
brigands who attacked the wayfarer might still have been lurking
in the immediate vicinity, awaiting the opportune moment to
waylay their next victim. Yet again, they might have entertained
suspicions that the man lying on the side of the roadway was
himself a would-be-robber who was engaged in a deadly game of
possum, patiently awaiting the opportunity to launch a surprise
attack against any would-be rescuer that approached him with the
intent of rendering first aid.[10] Employing his fertile imagination,
Dr. King surmised that the question both the priest and the Levite
asked themselves was, "If I stopped to help this man, what would
happen to me?" On the other hand, by the very nature of his concern, the Samaritan reversed the question, asking, "If I do not stop
to help this man, what would happen to him?"[11]

It is quite evident that Jesus took special pains to highlight
the ethnicity of the Samaritan in His telling of the enduring story.

Samaritans were viewed as a despised underclass by their Jewish brethren. In 722 BCE, the Assyrian army invaded the northern kingdom of Israel and decimated its capital, Samaria. After conquering the Jewish homeland, much of the populace was deported to Assyria, and foreigners were brought in to settle. Foreign civilians and Assyrian soldiers intermarried with Israelite women. Intermarriage between the two ethnic groups produced a mixed-race population that eventually departed from the orthodox tenets of the Jewish religion. They even established their own temple of worship at Mount Gerezim.

As time ensued, the population was derogatively branded with the name of Samaritans. They were so despised by their pure-blooded Jewish brethren in the south, that if the shadow of a Samaritan crossed the person of a Jew while they encountered each other on the street, the Jew would reckon him or herself to be ritually impure, and underwent a period of ritual cleansing in order to regain ritual purity. However, even though the Samaritan was aware of the fact that his Jewish brethren despised him, he still dispensed compassion to his wounded brother in several distinct ways.

The first way in which the Samaritan dispensed compassion to his wounded brother was by demonstrating courage. Even though he was aware of the fact that he was a "sitting duck" when he stopped on the crime-infested roadway to render assistance to his fallen comrade, the compassion welling up within his bosom compelled him to display courage. Unlike the priest and the Levite, who were both bound by religious conventions that prevented them from dispensing compassionate care to the suffering wayfarer, the Samaritan refused to be stymied by conventions that prevented him from stopping and ministering to someone in dire need of life-saving medical assistance.

The second way in which the Samaritan dispensed compassion to his wounded brother was by being a "ministering presence" in the face of tragedy, loss, and chaos, and demonstrating care about the wounded man's welfare. While the biblical narrative is silent on the actual ministrations that he dispensed to his bed-ridden brother during the long night while he was immersed in the drama of life and death, the care that he dispensed to him prevented the wounded soul from slipping over the precipice of suffering into death.

The third way the Samaritan dispensed compassion to his wounded brother was by demonstrating commitment to his predicament. And he did so by footing the full cost of the man's medical expenses. After rescuing his wounded brother, the Samaritan knew that he would need ample time to recuperate in order to recapture a semblance of full health. Since the robbers took all of the money that the wayfarer had on his person, he was incapable of footing his medical bills or meeting the financial obligations of his family. As such, the Samaritan covered the costs of his bills to ensure that he would not be burdened by the anxiety incurred by financial expenses.

The fourth way in which the Samaritan dispensed compassion to his wounded brother was by recognizing that he was created in the image and likeness God, and that the Spirit of God resided within his physical being. He recognized the wounded man's body as God's temple, a site of God's manifestation in the world, and the locus of divine activity. As such, he honored the man as a child of God by ensuring that he was restored to a full state of health.

The fifth way in which the Samaritan dispensed compassion to his wounded brother was by providing the man with a place of refuge where he could fall asleep in the presence of a loving, watchful gaze as he recuperated from his wounds. Even though his actions incurred unforeseen financial expenses, he suspended his business ventures in order to provide care to a total stranger.

After the children of Israel were settled in Canaan, God stipulated the establishment of cities of refuge (see Num. 35:6-32; Josh. 20:2-3; 21:13-38; 1 Chron. 6:67). The prophet Isaiah writes, *"For Thou hast been a strength to the poor, a strength to the needy in his distress, a refuge from the storm, a shadow from the heat, when the blast of the terrible ones is as a storm against the wall"* (Isa. 25:4). Throughout the Scriptures God demonstrated concern about the plight of refugees, the homeless, and the abandoned. Even though the wounded man might have been financially well off and the head of a family, he was at the time of his pain-predicament subjected to the very predicament individuals who are marginalized from the mainstream of society routinely experience. He was relegated to a state of physical and financial oppression, and left to die on the side of a dangerous highway. For all practical purposes, he was a refugee in need of a sanctuary that afforded him the opportunity to recuperate from his wounds. As such, the Samaritan provided him with a haven of refuge.

The Zulu people of South Arica subscribe to a worldview that is referred to by the African community as *ubuntu*. The core principle of the worldview embraces the belief that when the Spirit of God descended from heaven to earth, it established residence within the bodies of humankind. In the estimation of the Zulu people, every human being is a spark of the Divine. And in those instances when we dispense care and compassion to our brothers and sisters, we simultaneously dispense care and compassion to the Spirit of God embodied in human beings. By dispensing care and compassion to his wounded brother, the Samaritan not only demonstrated that his Jewish brother was created in the image and likeness of God—the *imago Dei*—it also indicated that the Spirit of God resided within him. As such, he unknowingly subscribed to the Zulu worldview of *ubuntu*.

Dr. King indicated that the Good Samaritan engaged in dangerous altruism when he stopped to render assistance to the wounded wayfarer, thereby exposing himself to potential danger.[12] It is also true that Mother Teresa and Paul Rusesabgina engaged in dangerous altruism when they exposed themselves to potential danger in order to care for individuals who were less fortunate than themselves. Jesus undoubtedly placed a high premium on the practice of dangerous altruism since He took special pains to include the parable of the so-called Good Samaritan in the body of teachings that He left as a legacy to humanity.

The dangerous altruism practiced by the three apostles of love is a demonstration of *agape* by individuals who availed themselves to God so that the Almighty might utilize them as tributaries of grace in ways that served to strengthen the bonds of brotherhood and sisterhood within the human family. The courageous actions of the three indicate that love is a verb—a dynamic pulsating activity that is congruent with the sentiments of M. Scott Peck, M.D., who believes that love is demonstrated through our exertion—through the fact that for someone (or for our self) we take an extra step or walk an extra mile. Love is not effortless. To the contrary, love is effortful.[13]

We Must Continue Loving Ourselves in Difficult Times Because God Loves Us

On those occasions when difficulties impact our lives, we are oftentimes besieged by questions pertaining to the origin of our suffering. It is not unusual for us to inquire as to why we are suffering the way we are, even though there are occasions when the answers to such questions appear hidden and not readily available to us. The prolonged questioning on our part and the perceived non-response on God's part further tend to heighten our anxieties. As such, we fail to be receptive to words of solace from heaven and fall prey to states of self-denigration, self-hatred, low self-esteem, and resignation. It could be argued that by taking refuge in these negative states, we unconsciously engage in acts of spiritual murder. In difficult times, when we are relegated to a maze of miseries and afflicted by anxiety and bitterness that tear at the fabric of our being, it is not uncommon for us to rail and shake our fists at God concerning our predicament. However, because it's His nature to do so, God accepts us and loves us, even in our hatefulness and vengefulness. C.S. Lewis counsels: "Lay before Him what is in us, not what ought to be in us."[14]

In providing us with an insightful perspective, David extols God's love for humankind with the declaration: *"How precious also are Thy thoughts unto me, O God! How great is the sum of them! If I should count them, they are more in number than the sand: when I awake, I am still with Thee"* (Ps. 139:17-18). In his journeying with God, David arrived at the heightened awareness that he was fearfully and wonderfully made (see Ps. 139:14). He recognized that in every life situation, God dispensed unconditional love toward him and brooded over him as a protective hen broods over her chicks. He further recognized that in whatever condition we might find ourselves, the Creator is never separated from us. David's insightful declaration brings home to us the reality of our preciousness to God. And, if we are precious to God, how could we possibly continue to live divided and diminished by self-denigration, self-hate, or low self-esteem?

Even though we might not be able to fully comprehend the magnitude of God's love for us on those occasions when adversity rakes us over the coals, God continues to love us despite the predicament in which we might find ourselves. God's love is unconditional of any condition. And because the Creator loves us in whatever condition we might be immersed, we must make every effort to continue loving ourselves. Simone Weil writes, "God's love for us is reason enough for us to love ourselves."[15] We must always remember that if God never abandons us, under no circumstances should we abandon ourselves; and we should continue to engage in pursuits that will help us reclaim a semblance of wholeness.

On those occasions when we are impacted by adversity, we are prone to buy into the mistaken assumption that if we were truly OK in God's eyes, He would not have permitted adversity to show up at our front door adorned in any of its various guises. The onset of adversity occasionally influences us to entertain the erroneous notion that God might have singled us out for misfortune. This mindset influences us to entertain the illusion that something must be wrong with us, since we are not as "perfect" as individuals that are free from tribulation. Therefore, we are the deserving recipients of the adversity impacting our life situation. But whether or not we are responsible for the difficulties impacting our lives, it does not mean that we should give up on loving ourselves. If the truth be told, it is in those instances when we are hobbled by self-inflicted wounds that we need to be extra vigilant about dispensing loving care to ourselves so that we might gather the requisite strength to recapture a semblance of wholeness. In very much the same way that we might have been instrumental in "wounding" ourselves, we must partner with God in dispensing healing to ourselves also.

During the brief three or so years of His earthly ministry, Jesus encouraged suffering folk to partner with Him in facilitating their recovery from illness, instructing them on occasion to stretch out a withered hand (see Matt. 12:10-13; Mark 3:1-5; John 6:6-11), or to take up their bed and walk (see Matt. 9:6; Mark 2:1-11; Luke 5:17-24). The exhortation that individuals should participate with Him in recapturing a semblance of wholeness indicates that God desires that we partner with Him in accruing much-desired healing to ourselves, because the Creator will not do for us that which we must do for ourselves.

Loving Ourselves in Difficult Times Is Indispensible to Recovery

Loving ourselves in difficult times is indispensible to our being restored to a semblance of wholeness, because it prevents us from pursuing destructive behaviors that serve to compound our pain-predicament and erode our sense of well-being. *Loving ourselves unconditionally enables us to stay focused on recovery and the acquisition of wholeness.* It also enables us to embrace the sentiments of the helpful idiom: "This too shall pass." Further still, it enables us to arrive at the firm understanding that through God's amazing grace, we will experience restoration to wholeness.

German theologian and philosopher Paul Tillich refers to grace as "the reunion of life with life, and the reconciliation of the self with itself."[16] In this vein, loving ourselves during difficult times prevents us from surrendering to the status quo and eventually giving up on life. It enables us to avail ourselves to God's grace by setting our sights beyond the pain-predicament impacting our lives, and envisioning the future as being pregnant with possibilities.

Grace has the power to transform fate into a meaningful destiny. It enables us to recognize that by means of God's unmerited favor, as grace is known, we are afforded a portal into the future through which we can visualize amazing possibilities with spiritual eyes. Loving ourselves during seasons of adversity imbues us with a renewed perspective for the future by enabling us to lay claim to the promises of God instead of becoming entrapped in the constricting grip of any predicament. Visualizing those things that are possible through faith enables us to lay claim to the biblical injunction: *"For I know the thoughts that I think toward you, saith the Lord, thoughts of peace, and not of evil, to give you an expected end"* (Jer. 29:11).

Loving Ourselves in Difficult Times Is a Sacred Obligation

Even though caregivers might provide us with needed support in those instances when we are impacted by difficult circumstances, we are still saddled with the sacred obligation of loving ourselves unconditionally, because our heavenly Father loves us unconditionally and desires to manifest Himself within our earthly temples to the fullest extent possible. The ancient idiom reminds us, "Charity begins at home." As such, we must make it a high priority to dispense charity within the precincts of our "home," i.e., by caring in all ways possible for our physical temples, despite the trials confronting us at any given point in time. Loving ourselves unconditionally acknowledges that even though we might be assailed by adversity, ultimately, our lives still matter and are worth fighting for. Our lives are worth fighting for because we are God's creation and workmanship—the apple of

His eye and the sheep of His pasture. *Even though life occasionally proves to be extremely painful, God remains eternally good.* And as long as our heavenly Father affords us the opportunity to remain on this side of eternity, it signifies that He has not yet completed the sacred task of transforming our life situation, despite the hellish forces that might be impacting our existence. Only when suffering souls develop the insight to embrace this liberating worldview will they be able to care for themselves in all ways necessary.

Recovery from difficult circumstances is contingent on the mental attitude of individuals consigned to the crucible of suffering. If suffering souls find it difficult to love themselves unconditionally, this mindset will have a negative impact on the recovery process because it will prevent them from mustering the energies needed to battle the forces degrading their well-being. On the other hand, if they love themselves unconditionally, it becomes a much easier task in summoning the resources needed to battle the attending adversity. *Medical research has concluded that adopting an optimistic outlook on life during bouts of illness has a positive effect on our immune system and plays an important role in helping our bodies in battling diseases.* Additionally, individuals possessing a high degree of self-love and a purpose for living stand a much better chance overcoming adversity as opposed to those who do not because they tend to have a positive outlook on the future. They envision life as something worth fighting for, and are better predisposed to do battle against the negative forces impacting their spirit, as opposed to individuals who do not have such an outlook on the future. Loving ourselves unconditionally when we are confronted with difficult circumstances is an indispensable ingredient of the recovery process.

Loving Ourselves in Difficult Times Is a Gateway to Healing

Loving ourselves unconditionally during difficult times is a gateway to healing. This is because it enables us to visualize ourselves as recipients of God's love, and become gateways through which the power and grace of God can enter our lives. This predisposition to healing affords the Holy Spirit the opportunity to inhabit us and work on our behalf. In a similar way, as Mary is referred to as the *theotokus*—the "God-bearer"—we are afforded the sacred opportunity of "bearing" or carrying God's Holy Spirit within our physical being. In the act of "bearing" the Holy Spirit, our bodies participate in *theosis* (realizing the divinity within).

The Holy Spirit ministers to us most effectively in an environment of love because God is holy love. So, despite the difficulties in which we might find ourselves at any given point in time, we are still afforded the opportunity to cultivate a climate of love by heeding God's admonition to love ourselves unconditionally. David exhorts us to embrace the truth that we are fearfully and wonderfully made (see Ps. 139:14). When we recognize our bodies as fleshy temples of Almighty God, we are better able to afford God's healing Spirit—*Jehovah Roephka*—the opportunity to inhabit us and render us the repositories of divine energies.

During difficult times, we are oftentimes subjected to pain that is accompanied by enormous amounts of mental energy. In such instances, we are prone to become crippled by the magnitude of the experience and entrapped in our misery. In other words, we unwittingly become inmates in a prison house of pain where we are the jailers holding the key to our prison cell. Loving ourselves unconditionally prevents us from wallowing in self-pity and feeling sorry for ourselves, to the extent that we give in to our problems because we assume that they are too much to handle, rendering us incapable of struggling to recapture a semblance of wholesomeness.

While we should never deny the reality of pain, loving ourselves unconditionally enables us to recognize that with God's help we can become empowered to mount a vigorous response against any kind of adversity that might assail us and, by so doing, break the chains that conspire to keep us entrapped in our pain-predicament. When we relinquish our circumstances to the sovereignty of God, not only will He avail us power to break out of our holding cell, He will also avail us insight to fight the good fight of faith; and He will provide us with a vision that is fraught with infinite possibilities, thereby motivating us to migrate from our prison house of pain to a place of restoration.

Loving ourselves unconditionally in difficult times enables us to acknowledge that pain is a universal phenomenon. This liberating insight prevents us from feeling singled out for punishment by God. And it prevents us from becoming hobbled by anger, helplessness, depression, and other negative states. *Loving ourselves unconditionally enables us to acknowledge our pain and losses, and visualize the proverbial glass of life as being half-full instead of half-empty.* It also enables us to cultivate an attitude of gratitude for those things which we have already attained during the strenuous recovery process, such as incremental, but albeit significant gains already realized in reclaiming a semblance of full health and well-being—things like available support systems, the determination to rebuild our lives, and the gift of God's availing grace for the living of our days. Cognitive psychologists recognize the wisdom of encouraging patients to identify the things they are grateful for as part of the recovery process of behavioral modification. This approach to recovery enables patients to capture glimmers of light in the enveloping darkness, thereby influencing them to shift their gaze from a dominant attitude of negativity to a more positive and helpful approach to their situation.

Loving ourselves unconditionally prevents us from trivializing the recovery process, reminding us that we ought to be vigilant about doing those things which we must do for ourselves instead of leaving everything to fate or God. In other words, we must engage in prophetic action. Loving ourselves is a volitional act—a dynamic process or alteration between life-diminishing and life-enhancing coping, where each day in the life of a sufferer is different, and no two days are exact replicas of each other.

Loving Ourselves Unconditionally Testifies to the Goodness of God

Loving ourselves unconditionally in difficult times gives us the opportunity of bearing witness to the truth that adversity need never have the last word over our life situation. Every individual is desirous of being the recipient of good news that avails him or her hope for the future. Suffering people tend to become emboldened by testimonials from individuals who were at one point in time encumbered by adversity, but who through God's availing grace were able to mount successful recoveries from their pain-predicament. Testimonials from former sufferers serve as potions of emotional octane that serve to boost the morale of individuals who are immersed in difficult circumstances. Testimonials from former sufferers additionally serve as missives that encourage suffering to maintain the ongoing struggle to eventually recapture a semblance of wholesomeness. It reminds them that, despite the forces of adversity that might be impacting their well-being, they are potential candidates for liberation. When we heed God's admonition to love ourselves unconditionally and maintain the struggle to recapture a semblance of wholeness, we unknowingly serve as ambassadors of our heavenly Father's ability to transform the most horrific life situation.

Loving Ourselves in Difficult Times Engenders Worship to God

The Bible is fraught with instances where individuals remained steadfast in their worship toward God even though they were assailed by difficulties of the worst kind. Scripture bears witness to the fact that love for God is not contingent on the state of human emotions. Instead, it is an affair of the will. If worship of the Creator ensued exclusively from our emotions, worship would cease when human emotions are spent. In truth, worship of the Creator ensues from an unshakeable faith in the goodness of God because God's love has been poured into our hearts. As such, we are able to practice love despite the conditions in which we might find ourselves.

David was immersed in difficult circumstances when he was on the run, hiding out from his jealous father-in-law in a cave in the city of Adullam. Lifting anthems of praise to heaven during his pain-predicament, the elusive quarry declared: *"I will bless the Lord at all times: His praise shall continually be in my mouth"* (Ps. 34:1). Like David, it proves to be extremely beneficial when we purpose in our heart to cultivate the spiritual maturity that attests to the truth that God is worthy of our worship at all times. Our heavenly Father is worthy of our worship during the midnight of despair. And He is worthy of our worship in the noontime of fulfillment. Even though our heavenly Father occasionally allows difficult circumstances to disrupt the tranquility of our lives, He is not desirous of punishing us, but merely recognizes the need to subject us to the fiery furnace of adversity that serves to temper our spiritual steel. Fiery ordeals serve to burn away unnecessary dross, forming and reforming us, in order that our heavenly Father might show us a more excellent way.

Reflecting on David's outlook on life, modern-day pilgrims ought to purpose in our heart to cultivate the capacity to ascribe worship to the Creator in all of life's circumstances because God is sovereign over every aspect of our life situation. Ascribing worship to the Creator despite the painful circumstances in which we find ourselves at any given time engenders spiritual growth because, when we choose to avail ourselves to the transforming power of the Holy Spirit, the life of God Himself indwells us. We eventually arrive at the understanding that the Almighty is bigger than any situation that might confront us on this side of glory. And He has the final say as to how our circumstances will ultimately turn out.

Spiritual growth is an indispensable ingredient of the Christian life. And it is the next rung of the ladder we are exhorted to grab hold of as we travel from the terrain of tragedy and turmoil to the threshold of triumph.

Reflection Questions

1. What practices are you engaged in that might help to deepen your capacity to practice *agape*?

2. What obstacles, if any, might be hindering you from cultivating the deepest possible levels of *agape*?

3. How has the biblical exhortation to love your neighbor as yourself influenced your daily actions and decisions?

CHAPTER SEVEN

Turn Difficulties Into Dividends

When given the opportunity to do so, difficult experiences oftentimes influence us to become estranged from God. On the other hand, they might be viewed as invitations whereby we might cultivate the deepest possible relationship with the Creator. Thomas Aquinas said of difficulties, as Aristotle said of shame, that it was a thing not good in itself; but a thing which might have certain goodness in particular circumstances.[1]

When we look to the Bible for concrete evidence supporting the premise that difficult experiences can be utilized as occasions that invite us to engage in pursuits that engender spiritual growth, the life of David is again referenced as a case study. After being compelled to flee the environs of Jerusalem in order to escape threats against his life by his jealous and demented father-in-law Saul, David hid out in the cave of Adullam, a refuge 13 miles southwest of Bethlehem, where his immediate family members were *"everyone who was in distress, and everyone who was in debt, and everyone who was discontented gathered to him; and he became captain over them"* (1 Sam. 22:2 NRSV).

Recognize Difficult Times As Opportunities to Bless God

From the time that he took up residency in the king's palace, to the onset of the life-threatening events that compelled him to flee the environs of Jerusalem, David lived a storybook existence. After slaying the Philistine giant, Goliath of Gath, in the Valley of Elah, and after being awarded the king's daughter Michal as a consolation prize for his defeat of the battle-hardened colossus, he became an occupant of the royal household and a member of the "upper crust" of society. Unfortunately, after falling out of the good graces of the insecure king, David lost his wife, his esteemed social status, and all of the amenities that came in tow with palace life. On account of the frayed relationship with his father-in-law, not only was his name unceremoniously stricken from the social register, he was relegated to the status of *persona non grata* from the precincts of the palace, and was now a fugitive outlaw hiding out in a dark cave in the company of a bunch of outlawed malcontents like himself.

For all practical purposes, the giant-slayer hit rock bottom when his world unraveled and collapsed around him like a flimsy house of cards. Instead of allowing the thunderstorm that was howling through his life to relegate him to a cosmos of despair and despondency, David utilized the pain-drenched predicament as the opportune event to center his affections on Almighty God. He recognized the ordeal impacting his life as the perfect opportunity to relinquish the nonentity and insufficiency of all other concerns and abandon his circumstances to the saving grace of his heavenly Father, confident that he could depend on the Creator's all-sufficiency to see him through the turbulent times.

Several biblical scholars share the consensus that it was during David's cave dwelling sojourn at Adullam that he received inspiration to pen the words of the beautiful 34th Psalm, beginning with the glorious affirmation: *"I will bless the Lord at all times; His praise shall continually be in my mouth"* (Ps. 34:1 NRSV). David's fall from grace was undoubtedly painful and precipitous, but instead of allowing the difficulties impacting his life to disrupt, disable, or derail his destiny, he surrendered his pain-predicament to God, allowing the Almighty the opportunity to utilize it to fashion him a new destiny from the fragments of his painful situation.

When we look at David's trials from a purely human perspective, there are skeptics who are inclined to believe that it was utterly impossible for him to "bless" God at a time when his life was spinning out of control and he had seemingly lost it all—position, prestige, privilege, patronage, and power. How could he possibly summon the resolve to bless God when he found himself languishing in dire straits, and his life hung precariously in the balance? There are undoubtedly those naysayers who are inclined to believe that he could not have been genuine in his motivations, and was merely pretending and putting on a show.

Ancient manuscripts reveal that the Hebrew word for *bless* that was employed by David on the occasion of the composition of the beautiful psalm is *bawrak*. The word denotes active adoration, meaning, "to kneel," "to offer praise," or "to salute." By offering up to God such a wonderful anthem of praise during the turbulent season of his life, David demonstrated that it was the perfect opportunity to turn his attention away from the difficulties darkening the horizons of his existence. And by so doing, he availed himself to the transcendent possibilities that are possible through the providence of Almighty God. David recognized that even though the circumstances in which he was immersed were not what he would have liked them to be, he remained resolute in visualizing possibilities that existed beyond the boundaries of the attending adversity. Because of this, he discovered God in the strength of his faith and remained steadfast in pressing forward to a new reality, simultaneously drawing succor and sustenance from Him who is all-sufficient and all-merciful—to Him who is *"all in all"* (1 Cor. 15:28 NRSV).

We Must Recognize God's Immanence in Difficult Times

In those instances when adversity washed over his life like a tidal wave, David utilized worship as the vehicle to transport himself into the presence of God's *shekinah* instead of allowing the difficulties impacting his life to estrange him from his Maker, and thus influencing him to shun the Creator's presence. From his youthful days as a shepherd boy, when he spent extensive amounts of time in solitude out in the windswept wilderness caring for his father's herd of sheep, to his installation as captain of troops in the king's palace, David cultivated the insight to recognize that God was present with him in the exhilarating heights and the depressing depths of his life experiences.

Writing in the 139th Psalm, he indicated that if he ascended to heaven, God would be there. Yet again, if he made his bed in hell, God would again be there. Further still, if he took the wings of the morning and dwelt in the uttermost parts of the sea, God would also be there (see Ps. 139:7-10). Writing on yet another occasion in the 23rd Psalm, David declared: *"Thou anointest my head with oil; my cup runneth over"* (Ps. 23:5). Anointing of the head was an exclusive rite that was traditionally reserved for kings, prophets, and honored guests at banquets. In those instances when David became subjected to the hammer blows of adversity, he somehow experienced God's anointing coursing through the precincts of his spirit, signifying that he was precious to the Creator. The comforting words of the beautiful psalm attest to the reality of an omnipresent God whose existence was insinuated in every facet of his life situation. The assurance of God's protective presence motivated the future king of Israel to bless the Creator despite the painful events that assailed him when he was mired in adversity.

Unfortunately, far too many people employ human emotions as the barometer to ascertain whether or not God is present with them in their life situation. When things appear to be going well, they experience a sense of well-being and conclude that the Almighty is present with them. On the other hand, when things are not going as well as they would like them to, they erroneously conclude that God had abandoned them. In truth, God is eternally present with us. He never intended that we employ human emotions as the acid test to signify His absence or presence in our life situation, because human emotions tend to be fickle.

Aligning our wills with the promises enshrined in God's word is the means whereby we receive the assurance that our heavenly Father is present with us. Scripture tells us that Jesus promised that He would be with us till the end of time (see Matt. 28:20). Erecting the foundations of his life on this reality prompted Paul to declare:

For I am persuaded, that neither death, nor life, nor
angels, nor principalities, nor powers, nor things present,
nor things to come, nor height, nor depth, nor any other
creature, shall be able to separate us from the love of God,
which is in Christ Jesus our Lord (Romans 8:38-39).

Like David, Paul recognized that while we might on occasion be inclined to feel separated from God during stormy episodes, Scripture bears witness to the truth that our heavenly Father is never separated from us because His very life sustains us. By becoming grounded in this reality, we are able to trust God completely and avail ourselves to His transforming power.

Jurgen Moltman was incarcerated as a prisoner of war in Nazi Germany during World War II. During his detention in the penal obscenity, he was subjected to excruciating difficulties, and compelled to subsist on meager rations of poor food. With ample time on his hands in which to engage in personal reflection, he daily struggled with the reality of his country's miserable failings and the impending defeat of Adolf Hitler's evil regime by the combined armies of the Allied forces.

During his stretch of imprisonment, he had in his possession poems of Johann Wolfgang von Goethe, and the writings of Friedrich Wilhelm Nietzsche. In addition to the literature of his fellow countrymen, he began reading the New Testament in earnest. As a result of his daily meditations on Scripture, he experienced a spiritual transformation at the core of his being, and came to know Jesus as his personal and indwelling Savior. After being liberated from his prison house of pain, Moltman wrote in vivid detail about his spiritual rebirth: "I saw how other men collapsed inwardly, how they gave up all hope, sickening for the lack of it, some of them dying. The same almost happened to me. What kept me from it was a rebirth to a new life, thanks to a hope for which there is no evidence at all."[2]

Because of a personal encounter with the resurrected Lord of the New Testament that radicalized him at the very core of his being, Moltman was able to draw succor and sustenance from the life of Almighty God while being relegated to his life-withering experience in a cold and confining German prison cell.

We Must Recognize Difficult Times As Seasons of Spiritual Pruning

During the brief three or so years with His disciples, Jesus frequently employed helpful metaphors to unpack His principles and frame the relationship that He had cultivated with the motley crew of Galilean fishermen. One of the useful metaphors that the Teacher employed entailed Him being a vine, and His disciples the branches. In a similar manner, as vinedressers prune vines in vineyards assigned to their care, Jesus put His disciples on notice that they would likewise be subjected to seasons of pruning by His heavenly Father, who is the heavenly Vinedresser.

During seasons of pruning, vinedressers skillfully cut away dead, broken, damaged, and non-productive branches from vines so that the surging energy of the vines might be channeled into sturdy growth-producing branches. To individuals unfamiliar with the benefits of the pruning process, it might appear to be an exercise that is detrimental to the vines. However, after centuries of horticultural insight, vinedressers are intimately familiar with the positive outcomes that ensue from the pruning endeavors they engaged in. When we observe a pruned vineyard, we might be inclined to believe that it is highly unlikely that it would ever yield fruit at some point in the future. However, when the harvest finally arrives, we are brought to the realization that the process of pruning served as preparation instead of punishment.

In those instances when we are subjected to spiritual pruning by the hand of God, we might be inclined to entertain the notion that our heavenly Father is punishing us. Unknown to us, however, God is subjecting us to His refining process to enhance our growth potential as we journey the path to spiritual maturity. As spiritual vines, God desires that we shed non-productive aspects of our makeup that dissipate our spiritual energies in order that we are rendered capable of producing the maximum quota of spiritual fruit. To accomplish this feat, it is sometimes necessary that we be subjected to His heavenly pruning shears, which occasionally proves to be a painful exercise. But our heavenly Father often utilizes pain as a means of engendering our spiritual growth. While we might be inclined to view seasons of pruning as unmerited suffering, God is intimately familiar with methods of pruning that are beneficial to our spiritual growth. He desires that we develop robust spiritual lives with roots burrowing deep into the soil of His divine love. And His pruning shears are the tool He employs to shape us into His image and likeness, providing us with a deepened understanding and commitment to the faith.

We Must Recognize Difficult Times As Occasions for Reflection

There are instances when the pain-predicament in which we are immersed might very well ensue from wounds that are self-inflicted. It is therefore necessary to engage in prayerful reflection and ask God to reveal to us any destructive pursuits that we might be engaged in or that might be the root cause of our pain-predicament. In those instances when the Holy Spirit reveals sin to us, we need to acknowledge and forsake the besetting sin and seek God's forgiveness in order that we might be reestablished in a right relationship with Him. Additionally, we should ask God to furnish us with power to abandon our pain-generating pursuits.

Forgiveness is essential to our being established in a right relationship with God, because sin separates us from the Almighty and hinders the deepest possible relationship with our heavenly Father. We cannot engage in true worship with the Creator until such time that we align our lives with the principles enshrined in His word and are able to place ourselves in His presence cleansed from besetting sin. The psalmist was intimately aware of this truth when he wrote: *"If I regard iniquity in my heart, the Lord will not hear me: but verily God hath heard me; He hath attended to the voice of my prayer"* (Ps. 66:18-19). Corroboration of this reality is provided on another occasion in the writings of the prophet Isaiah: *"But your iniquities have separated between you and your God, and your sins have hid His face from you, that He will not hear"* (Isa. 59:2).

Seasons of reflection give us the opportunity to engage in watchfulness over our lives—to "set our house in order." They afford us the opportunity to be vigilant about keeping God enthroned at the center of our existence, where we are able to live from that center instead of attempting to live from life-negating sources that are incapable of offering abundant life. At some point on our life's journey, we inevitably arrive at the realization that true life is only found in God. And that the great reward of life is

God Himself. Ignorance of this reality is the prime reason many of us live in constant danger of being subjected to spiritual starvation, as noted by Simone, not because there is no bread, but because we have persuaded ourselves that we are not hungry.[3]

C.S. Lewis concurs with Weil's insightful assessment when he writes: "God gives what He has, not what He has not. To be God—to be like God and not share His goodness in creaturely response—to be miserable—these are the only three alternatives. If we will not learn to eat the only food that the universe grows— the only food that any possible universe can ever grow—then we must starve eternally."[4] Reflection prevents us from falling prey to spiritual anemia because it enables us to remain cognizant of the sources from which we seek spiritual food.

In like manner, as airline pilots are constantly engaged in the critical activity of re-attuning the course heading of aircrafts in order to keep the air ships on designated flight paths, reflection presents us with opportunities to engage in ongoing actions that prevent us from straying from our God-ordained trajectory. It is not unusual for us to occasionally behave like the prodigal son, and stray into some "far country" where we chase after things that are elusive and unsatisfying, eventually finding ourselves feeding on husks that are spiritually unfulfilling and non-life-giving (see Luke 15:11-32). But even in those instances when we foolishly undertake exhausting excursions into some "far country," the Good Shepherd seeks us out, and, after finding us, we are returned to our Father's house where we are clothed in robes of righteousness and established in a state of abundant life. *Being restored to our Father's house is the great spiritual journey Augustine spoke about when he declared, "You have made us for Yourself, and our heart is restless until it rests in You, O God."*[5]

We Must Recognize Difficult Times As Opportunities to Surrender to God's Will

There are instances when God subjects us to bitter experiences that we might recognize the wisdom of surrendering to His perfect will. While it is true that our heavenly Father occasionally affords us a certain amount of latitude by granting us His permissive will, the time eventually arrives when He insists that we submit to the dictates of His perfect will, that His divine purpose might be made evident in our lives. To make this a reality in our lives, He subjects us to difficult experiences so we might recognize the folly of indulging in misguided pursuits.

The four short chapters of the Book of Jonah chronicle the bitter experiences of the Hebrew prophet whose disobedience set him on a collision course with God's will when he ignored the divine directive. The Old Testament report indicates that God instructed Jonah to proceed to the Assyrian city of Nineveh. And his assignment after arriving at the ancient location entailed that of preaching repentance to the Assyrian people, that they might escape destruction by the hand of God.

As previously mentioned, the northern kingdom of Israel was swallowed up by the Assyrian empire in 722 BCE, when the Assyrian army decimated its capital city, Samaria, thereby establishing a wide chasm of hostility between the two nations. The ensuing tribal fault lines were palpable, coloring Jonah's attitude toward the imperial ambitions of Israel's archenemy, Assyria. Additionally, Jonah was intimately aware of the fact that Ninevites were pagan worshippers that were not included in the covenant nation of Jehovah God as the descendants of Abraham reckoned themselves to be. In lieu of this reality, he experienced difficulty being reconciled to the fact that the God of the ancient Hebrew patriarchs saw fit to bestow grace on "heathens," saving them from destruction.

Consumed by the pursuit of his misguided agenda, Jonah fled to the ends of the earth to forestall any possibility that the Ninevites would ever be afforded the opportunity to repent. On account of his disobedient actions, Jonah encountered calamity that resulted in him being unceremoniously dumped into the sea by the crew of the ship on which he attempted to evade God's directive. After being dumped into the turbulent waters, he was swallowed by a large fish in whose gut he remained imprisoned for three horrific days. On the third day of his undersea imprisonment, he was disgorged by the sea creature at the exact location from which he was instructed by God to embark on his divine assignment. After discerning that God was orchestrating the difficulties to which he had been subjected, Jonah recognized the imperative of surrendering to the Creator's will. Not only did his surrendering afford God's purpose to be accomplished as it pertained to the salvation of the Assyrian nation, it also afforded Jonah the opportunity to realign his will with God's will. It also created for him the opportunity to shed his prejudice and recognize the inclusiveness of all creation within the ambit of God's amazing grace.

We occasionally end up spinning our wheels, engaging in pursuits that encumber us with unnecessary hardships in those instances when we refuse to align our will with God's will. Just like our ancestral parents, Adam and Eve, we at times become afflicted with stubborn streaks of self-will and embrace the illusion that ultimately we know what is best for us. As such, we latch on to the controls of our lives with an unrelenting grip, refusing to entrust our circumstances to God so He might establish us on our divine trajectory. On those occasions when we refuse to abandon our self-willed ideations to God's providence, our heavenly Father deems it necessary to subject us to episodes of holy disillusionment to recognize the wisdom of surrendering our circumstances to His providence. Our involvement in acts of self-will blinds us to the reality that God has our best interest at heart, and that He is eternally predisposed to promoting our welfare. The imperative of surrendering our lives to the providence of Almighty God is reflected in the words of the Danish philosopher and theologian Soren Kierkegaard, when he declared: "What a man achieves or does not achieve is not within his power. He is not the One who shall steer the world; he has one and only one thing to do—obey."[6]

We Must Recognize Difficult Times As Seasons for Cross-Bearing

Jesus makes it crystal clear that there will be instances when we will be compelled to take up our cross and suffer in a similar manner as He did (see Matt. 10:38; 16:25). These are hard words to the ears of a world bent on pursuing success-oriented, materialistic, and a pain-free brand of spirituality. Pundits of success-oriented spirituality entice us to engage in spiritual cherry picking, where we selectively embrace passages of Scripture that are palatable to our consumption and ignore those that are painful to swallow and difficult to digest. But while words of joy and happiness hook our minds, sooner or later we will be compelled to grapple with words attesting to the truth that, as disciples of the Great Galilean, we will be compelled to take up our cross and partake of our Lord's suffering.

Scripture puts us on notice that cross-bearing is woven into the tapestry of our faith journey. Because of this, our heavenly Father occasionally encumbers us with personal crosses, causing us to become "wounded healers" resonating with the pain impacting the lives of suffering souls the world over. God also at times deems it necessary to encumber us with personal crosses in order that we might work toward the manifestation of the kingdom that can only come with *"godly grief...that leads to salvation"* (2 Cor. 7:10 NRSV). Writing on another occasion, Paul reminds us that we are children, indeed heirs of God and co-heirs with Christ *"if, in fact, we suffer with Him so that we may also be glorified with Him"* (Rom. 8:17 NRSV).

We Must Recognize Difficult Times As Pathways to Transformation

The objective of the Christian life is spiritual transformation. And our spiritual pilgrimage is one in which we have been summoned to transformation by our heavenly Father. *Embedded within our genetic code for eternity is God's program of spiritual transformation, where we mature and approximate the image and likeness of our risen Lord.* Episodes of adversity are not always meant for our destruction but to foster our spiritual maturity. C.S. Lewis contends that God oftentimes employs trouble as a means to "force us up" so we might become much braver, more patient, or more loving than we ever dreamed of before. He argues that it all may appear unnecessary at times, but we do not have the slightest notion of the tremendous thing God means to make of us.[7]

Physicians frequently cut and clean out infected wounds so that the wounds might become free of dead and diseased tissue cells, thereby creating aseptic conditions that are conducive to healing. While the process of cleaning wounds does occasionally prove to be a painful undertaking for patients, it is an indispensable aspect of medical treatment protocol. In very much the same way that physicians cut and clean out infected wounds, the Great Physician occasionally recognizes the need to utilize His spiritual scalpel to cut away negative aspects of our life situation in order that we might experience healing and regeneration in all aspects of our being.

Even though spiritual pruning is oftentimes painful, our heavenly Father recognizes the need to perform divine surgery within us to eliminate aspects of our makeup that hinder healing and transformation from taking place in our lives. C. S. Lewis concurs with this insightful sentiment, stating:

> We were not made primarily that we might love God
> (though we were made for that too) but that God might
> love us, that we might become the objects in which the
> Divine love may rest "well pleased." To ask that God's
> love should be content with us as we are, is to ask that
> God should cease to be God: because He is what He is,
> His Love must, in the nature of things, be impeded and
> repelled by certain stains in our present character, and
> because He already loves us He must labor to make
> us lovable.[8]

Several biblical references highlight the experiences of sages, saints, and ordinary folk who were compelled to endure seasons of adversity that were fraught with perceptions of forsakenness and insecurity, referred to by the spiritual masters as "the dark night of the soul." Despite the difficulties that prompted these individuals to wail in agony when adversity registered its painful one-two-punch to their spiritual solar plexus, the embattled souls responded to the trials confronting them with an answer from above instead of an answer from below. This orientation to life enabled them to remain receptive to a word from the dimension of the eternal, as evidenced in the life of the Old Testament prophet Habakkuk, who, while subjected to a tumultuous episode in his life, declared:

> *Although the fig tree shall not blossom, neither shall fruit*
> *be in the vines; the labour of the olive shall fail, and the*
> *fields shall yield no meat; the flock shall be cut off from*
> *the fold, and there shall be no herd in the stalls: yet I will*
> *rejoice in the Lord, I will joy in the God of my salvation.*
> *The Lord God is my strength, and He will make my feet like*
> *hinds' feet, and He will make me to walk upon mine high*
> *places* (Habakkuk 3:17-19).

The prophet recognized that in those instances when life became a barren desert and refused to blossom, God alone was his source of strength—his assurance. He recognized that when life became topsy-turvy, causing him to lose his spiritual equilibrium, God would provide him with *"hinds' feet."* Hinds, or deer as they are commonly known, are endowed by the Creator with cloven hooves that are extremely adept at navigating unstable and treacherous terrain. Deer possess the uncanny ability of placing their rear hooves in the exact spot from which they removed their front hooves while moving forward, thereby ensuring that they will continue to navigate on safe terrain. Even though the Old Testament prophet painted a scenario of gloom and doom in which he was immersed on the occasion of the ancient writing, he remained determined to respond to his perplexing dilemma with an answer from above instead of an answer from below, because he recognized God as the source of power and who was capable of transforming his life circumstances.

Despite the harsh realities impacting the life situation of the biblical wise one, Habakkuk experienced tranquility at the very core of his being because he determinedly looked to heaven for the resolution of his problem situation. His confidence resonated with the sentiments of the prophet Jeremiah, who declared: *"Stand ye in the ways, and see, and ask for the old paths, where is the good way, and walk therein, and ye shall find rest for your souls"* (Jer. 6:16). In order that we might be rendered capable of submitting ourselves to the trajectory of the ancient paths, our hearts must be wholly consumed by love for Almighty God.

John Mogabgab, former assistant to the late Henri Nouwen, informs us that love is the great magnet whose force field turns all things in its direction, aligning them toward an end they do not possess in themselves. However, to acknowledge love's pull upon us, and to allow love's sway to turn us toward our source, is the essence of prayer and the sure path of those who seek the good way.[9] Prayer is the next rung on the ladder we are exhorted to grab hold of as we make our way from the turbulent waters of life to an oasis teeming with tranquility.

Reflection Questions

1. After reading this chapter, how might you best employ difficult experiences as a means of enhancing your spiritual formation?

2. In your estimation, which biblical personalities utilized difficult experiences as a means to deepening their relationship with God?

3. Do you interpret bitter experiences to mean that we are being punished by God?

CHAPTER EIGHT

Practice Prayer
in Difficult Times

The great 19th-century Russian spiritual guide Theophan the Recluse indicated that prayer is the "test of everything, the source of everything, the driving force of everything, and the director of everything. The wise one concluded that if prayer is right, everything is right."[1]

The transformation engendered in the lives of human beings through the practice of prayer establishes the ancient discipline as an indispensible ingredient in the process of spiritual formation and the means whereby we engage in communion with the very heart of God. Southern Baptist philosopher and spiritual guide Dallas Willard accurately placed his finger on it with the insightful statement: "Prayer, it is rightly said, is the method of genuine theological research, the method of understanding who God is."[2] Willard indicates that above all, prayer is a means of forming character, and combines freedom and power with service and love. He contends that what God gets out of our lives and, indeed, what we get out of our lives is simply the person we become.

He concludes that it is God's intention that we grow into the kind of person He can empower to do what we want to do.[3] Providing us with yet another insightful perspective on the issue of prayer, Henri Nouwen said, *"Prayer is not a pious decoration of life but the breath of existence."*[4]

If we are honest with ourselves, we might admit that the practice of prayer under normal circumstances does not come easily. A large majority of us demonstrate ambivalence toward the practice of the ancient discipline. Our obsession with the *muchness* and *manyness* in modern life frequently leaves us waving to God as we frantically rush by on a daily basis in relentless pursuit of our enlightened self-interests. In addition to the endless litany of demands that crowd our daily agendas, we are confronted with yet another formidable challenge. During attempts to engage in meaningful prayer sessions with the Almighty, recalcitrant thoughts race through our minds, conspiring to drag us away from much-needed communion with our heavenly Father. That is why it is imperative that we recognize that the cultivation of disciplined prayer habits amid the seductions of modern life that vie for our attention is hard work. It involves being intentional about structuring quality time into our crowded agendas as periods dedicated to seeking encounters with the Lover of our souls. Even though strenuous, it eventually proves to be a rewarding endeavor leading to life in its fullest and finest sense.

Throughout His earthly existence, Jesus placed an extremely high premium on the practice of prayer. In much the same way as the exemplars of faith who trekked across the pages of the Bible in times past, our Lord's life was marinated with prayer. Prayer was the native language of His spirit. And before undertaking an important task, the very first thing He did was pray and seek His heavenly Father's counsel on the matter. Prayer held such a high priority on His daily agenda that He rose early in the morning to pray (see Mark 1:35), spent entire nights in prayer (see Luke 21:37), climbed a mountain to pray (see Matt. 14:23), entered a garden in order to pray (see Mark 14:36), took an excursion into the desert (see Luke 4:1), and relaxed in a boat far away from the seashore (see Matt. 14:13) so that He could distance Himself from the requests of the demanding crowd, finding the quietude whereby He might engage in communion with His heavenly Father. *The intentionality of structuring time for prayer in His daily agenda demonstrates that for our Lord prayer was a lived truth.* Not only did He place a high premium on prayer, but He also recognized the imperative of teaching His disciples the art of prayer (see Matt. 6:9-12).

Prayer Is Ordained by God

The Bible indentifies prayer as a discipline that is ordained by God. Paul's exhortation to the church at Thessalonica states: *"Pray without ceasing, give thanks in all circumstances; for this is the **will** of God in Christ Jesus for you"* (1 Thess. 5:17-18 NRSV). Paul's exhortation signifies that prayer is a spiritual discipline that is willed by God. Revealing congruent sentiments with those of the apostle, German martyr and Lutheran minister Dietrich Bonhoffer indicates that, *"Prayer is not a free-will offering to God; it is an obligatory service, something which he requires."*[5]

The sentiments of both luminaries of the Christian faith send a clear message to modern-day disciples of the Great Galilean that prayer is much more than a casual ritual that we engage in. To the contrary, prayer affords us the opportunity to cultivate an enduring fellowship with God on the most intimate basis possible. From a biblical perspective, prayer is the divinely established doorway through which believers move from the "outer court" to the "inner court"—the *qodesh qodashim* ("holy of holies" in Hebrew) of the spiritual realm—in order to engage in sacred communion with Jehovah God. Further still, prayer is the means whereby we make known our deep and pressing concerns to Him as we simultaneously listen with a spirit of receptivity to what He is saying to us.

God Is Receptive to the Prayers of His People

Despite the fact that a large segment of society demonstrates a high level of ambivalence toward the practice of prayer, the Bible indicates that God responds to the prayers of His people. Examples culled from Second Chronicles and the Book of Acts of the Apostles bear witness to this truth. The Bible declares: *"If My people, which are called by My name, shall humble themselves, and **pray**, and seek My face, and turn from their wicked ways; then will I hear from heaven, and will forgive their sin, and will heal their land"* (2 Chron. 7:14). It is evident from the biblical record that God responds to the prayers of His people. And it is one of the means whereby the Almighty makes His desires known to His creation in order that His divine purpose might be accomplished on earth. It is a means whereby we are able to experience transformation of our life situation because it spiritually connects us with God, enabling us to receive impartation from Him.

Writing in Acts of the Apostles, Luke chronicles the midnight liberation of Paul and Silas from the confining corridors of a Philippian jail after the evangelists were arrested and incarcerated for preaching the emerging and controversial Gospel of Jesus Christ within the precincts of the Macedonian town. Luke writes:

*About midnight Paul and Silas were **praying** and singing*
hymns to God, and the prisoners were listening to them.
Suddenly there was an earthquake, so violent that the
foundations of the prison were shaken; and immediately
all the doors were opened and everyone's chains were
unfastened (Acts 16:25-26 NRSV).

Untold scores anxiously wring their hands and lament their
predicament when they are assailed by adversity because they
are unaware of the efficacy of the established method for transforming their life situation. They are ignorant of the transformation that could accrue to them when they choose to pray to God
about their situation. Paul and Silas's response to the onset of adversity indicated that they were aware of the divine prescription
for engendering the transformation of life's oppressive situations.

Even though they were confronted with hardships, the apostles refused to bemoan their predicament and chose instead to
pray about it. They stretched their gaze beyond the confines of the
dark dungeon in which they were incarcerated by latching on to
the possibilities that are available through the practice of prayer.
The two pioneers of the Christian faith were aware of the fact that
God responds to the prayers of His creation despite the circumstances in which they might be immersed at any given point in
time. So, instead of commiserating about how bad their situation
was, they employed the divine formula that ought always to be
utilized in life's confining moments—lifting their voices to God
in anthems of praise and thanksgiving. They engaged in what the
Spanish mystic John of the Cross referred to as passive loving receptivity—leaning toward God in faith with longing, openness,
and love.[6] As God always does when suffering people pour out
their hearts into the ear of heaven, He liberated them from their

prison house of pain, thereby demonstrating that no fortress in the universe is impregnable enough to keep His beloved children in bondage when they seek liberation from oppressive situations by the practice of prayer.

Prayer Readies Us for Union With the Holy Spirit

It is utterly impossible to receive a word from the dimension of the eternal if we are not receptive to what our heavenly Father is saying to us. When our spirit is not attuned in the directives of God, it becomes difficult to discern the heavenly voice because the clamor of competing distractions tend to drown out His initiatives from reaching us, rendering us oblivious to what He is trying to convey to us.

As a radio receiver is able to capture signals from a transmitting station when the receiver is tuned to the frequency of the facility, in like manner we will only be able to hear from God when we are attuned to the heavenly siren call. The practice of prayer establishes a spiritual channel whereby we become predisposed to our heavenly Father in an attitude of receptivity, affording Him the opportunity to give us impartation in whatever way He deems fit. *By opening ourselves to God, we become conduits of the Holy that enables Him to impart His Spirit to us in full measure so we might be fashioned into a home for God in this world.* Prayer places us on a spiritual wavelength by which we become channels of grace and mercy that reverberate with the supernatural energies of God.

As we become more disciplined in the practice of prayer, we become sensitive to the "inner voice" that provides us with directives for the living of our days. The heightening of our spiritual acuity enables us to discern those instances when God is speaking to us, even when we are not engaged in the "drill" of formal or ritual prayer sessions. When our spiritual acuity becomes heightened to the point that we live in unbroken communication with our heavenly Father, we will be able to discern when He is speaking to us in what might be considered routine experiences.

God might choose to speak to us through a book. He might choose to speak to us through specific events, or He might choose to speak to us through particular individuals. God is always speaking to His children. However, we can only recognize when He is speaking by means of discernment when we are attuned to the "inner voice." And this is accomplished by the sanctifying action of the Holy Spirit when we surrender the nerve center of our consent to the transforming life of God. Percy C. Ainsworth declares: "Prayer is not merely claiming a hearing; it is giving a hearing. It is not only speaking to God; it is listening to God."[7]

It is evident that in order to receive a word from the dimension of the eternal, we must be sensitive to those instances when God is attempting to capture our attention. When we approach prayer with a casual attitude instead of being fully receptive to the heavenly voice, it hinders our communication with God the Father. It is imperative that we examine our conscience before engaging in prayer to be absolutely sure that God is our consuming passion and that no competing distractions will hinder our petitions from falling on a receptive ear.

Prayer Acquaints Us With God's Will

During His night of travail in the Garden of Gethsemane, Jesus prayed to His heavenly Father concerning His Abba's will for His life. Traumatized by the anguish ensuing from the knowledge of His rapidly approaching crucifixion on Calvary, our Lord prayed that, if possible, the cup of death that He was destined to drink to its bitter dregs might pass from Him. However, after recognizing that relinquishing the bloody chalice would derail God's redemptive plan, He appended His request with the surrendering prayer: *"Nevertheless not what I will, but what Thou wilt"* (Mark 14:36). Prayer was the medium through which our Lord received clarification concerning His Father's will for His life.

During episodes of adversity, it is not unusual for us to experience inner conflict concerning the best course of action that we should pursue to attain resolution of some painful dilemma. It is understandable that in the attempt to avoid additional increments of pain, we frequently tend to opt for the path of least resistance. Pursuing the path of least resistance might not necessarily provide us with the best possible resolution to our pain-predicament, however. Physicians prescribe medicine for patients that oftentimes prove to be distasteful to them. And patients, at times, buy into the erroneous assumption that the physicians are seeking to do them additional harm, only to discover at a later point in time that the prescription turned out to be their salvation. In very much the same way that patients are required to ingest medicine that is distasteful, the pathway culminating in problem resolution might entail opting for choices that subject us to additional bouts of hardship. The human tendency to avoid additional increments of pain influences us to shy away from making difficult choices even though they ultimately result in problem resolution. In such instances, prayer opens us up to impartation from God that avails us insight concerning the best course of action that we ought to pursue in those times when we are confronted with episodes of misty uncertainty.

When we align our will with God's divine will, our heavenly Father will endue us with the power to cope with the difficulties of life as we climb our steep hill of recovery that culminates in problem resolution. God is intimately familiar with the threshold of pain each of His children is able to endure. And He is intimately familiar with the circumstances attending every pathway we are compelled to traverse on this side of glory. When we submit to His divine will, He will give us insight as to how we ought to navigate through the trials in which we are immersed. The psalmist reminds us that God is our rock and our fortress, and He is our strong deliverer (see Ps. 139:12).

We Must Always Pray in the Name of Jesus

In far too many instances, we fail to experience transformation of our life situation because we fail to pray in the right way—thus our prayers usually amount to nothing more than empty rituals lacking spiritual grip or a firm understanding of the state of mind with which we ought to approach the throne of grace. Ignorance of the mindset with which we ought to approach the throne of grace becomes problematic in those instances when we are confronted with difficult circumstances. Instead of relying on the power of God to bring about transformation of our life situation, our desperation to experience liberation from our pain-predicament frequently influences us to indulge in emotional rants that merely render us frustrated, fatigued, and unresponsive to the Holy Spirit instead of providing us with the assurance that our petitions are reaching the courts of the heavenly King. The Bible tells us that when we pray in the name of Jesus, we have the assurance that our prayers will be answered because the Holy Spirit responds to our petitions, works *through* us, and imparts insight concerning resolution of our problem situation.

Praying in the name of Jesus entails much more than arbitrarily invoking the Savior's name as if it were a magic incantation. And it is much more than heaping up empty phrases and tagging on our Lord's name at the conclusion of our petition, expecting that something miraculous will happen. The Bible tells us that we ought to pray in the name of Jesus with the full assurance that our heavenly Mediator will respond to our prayers. While we are not privy as to how God works things out in the spiritual realm, we could rest assured that when we pray to Jesus, the hosts of heaven are mobilized to work on behalf of God's children to provide us with answer to our prayers.

Gerrit Scott Dawson informs us that in Trinitarian language, the whole journey of our prayer takes place within the life of Almighty God. When we pray, the Holy Spirit, who prays through our spirit, makes known our petitions to the eternal Son seated at the right hand of our heavenly Father. The Son receives our petitions, makes them His very own, and presents them, now cleansed and sanctified, to His Father. The Father, who delights in answering the prayers of the Son, responds, and the Son, in turn, pours out the Spirit in greater measure to us. Our prayers are answered according to the will of the Triune God.[8] Dawson presents us with the imagery of a symbolic way of expressing true reality that is beyond human description. He does indicate, however, that because of who God is, He does not need to wait to hear our prayers via the Spirit and the Son to know what we have prayed for. For the Triune God, all creation is simultaneously and equally present in the divine awareness.[9]

We Must Rely on the Power of the Holy Spirit

In far too many instances, the expected results of prayer tend to center on the spiritual "qualifications" of the one praying.

Instead of relying on the efficacy or power of the Holy Spirit that is operative in our midst, expected results of prayer unfortunately tend to center on human efforts. By tying expected outcomes of prayer to human ability, we fail to heed the admonition of the ancient prophet: *"Not by might, nor by power, but by **My** Spirit saith the Lord of hosts"* (Zech. 4:6). From a biblical perspective, prayer requires the life and work of Christ the Mediator in order to be effective. And our link with Christ is the Holy Spirit, who has been placed within us by our heavenly Father so we may engage in communion with Him and have our prayers answered. Employing the language of computer technology in our efforts to better understand this reality, someone referred to the Holy Spirit as the "operating system" of the believer's life. For added emphasis, it could also be said that the Holy Spirit is the "power plant" of the believer's life.

During His life on earth, Jesus lived in total submission to the dictates of the Holy Spirit. As it pertained to His humanity, He was first and foremost a man of the Spirit. Scripture indicates that God in the person of Jesus donned the garb of human flesh and dwelt among us (see John 1:14). Luke indicates that on the occasion of our Lord's baptism in the river Jordan, the Spirit descended upon Him mightily in the form of a dove as He emerged from the refreshing waters, and He was filled with the Spirit to preach good news and heal the sick (see Luke 1:35; 3:22; 4:14). The same Spirit led Him into the barren wilderness where He was tempted by the Adversary, and where He was also sustained by the very Spirit throughout His desert trials (see Luke 4:1). Additionally, the Spirit was present with Him in the darkness of Gethsemane on the night before His crucifixion on Calvary (see Luke 22:39-46). And yet again, it was through the power of the Spirit that He accomplished the ultimate sacrifice of surrendering His life on a crude Roman instrument of execution in order to make atonement for sinful humanity. It was also through the power of the Spirit that He was miraculously raised back to life on the third day after being crucified on Calvary (see Heb. 9:14; Rom. 8:11; 1 Pet. 3:18).

From the above references, it is quite evident that the power of the Holy Spirit permeated every aspect of the Messiah's life, and everything belonging to the Spirit belongs to the Son. This truth is corroborated by the words of John, who states, *"Howbeit when He, the Spirit of truth, is come, He will guide you into all truth: for He shall not speak of Himself; but whatsoever He shall hear, that shall He speak: and He will shew you things to come. He shall glorify Me: for He shall receive of mine, and shall shew it unto you"* (John 16:13-14).

Even though Jesus is physically absent from the material realm, the Holy Spirit continues to be active in our midst. Before His return to heaven, our Lord informed His disciples that He would send the Comforter to them so that they would receive knowledge concerning all things (see John 14:26). Paul tells us that God's love is poured into our hearts through the Holy Spirit who is imparted to every believer (see Rom. 5:5). He indicated on another occasion that God pours the Holy Spirit into our hearts, causing us to cry, "Abba, Father" (see Rom. 8:15). He writes yet again that the Holy Spirit bears witness with our spirit that we are children of God, and prays on our behalf—God praying to God— with groaning and utterings that are far too deep for words (see Rom. 8:16,26).

Numerous biblical references highlight the fact that through the mediatory office of the ascended Christ, we are ushered by prayer into our heavenly Father's presence by the active work of the primordial Holy Spirit—*rûach* in Hebrew and Aramaic. The Holy Spirit continues the work of creation and re-creation in our world in very much the same way He did while moving across the face of the waters at the time of creation (see Gen. 1:2). The Holy Spirit is God's agent whereby God's "new thing" becomes a reality in the lives of those who through Christ choose to entrust their circumstances to His providential care.

It is evident from the biblical record, that since the Holy Spirit prays on our behalf, we are ultimately not the ones who are in control. While we *do* need to be intentional about structuring quality time in our daily schedules for the practice of prayer, ultimately prayer is a divine encounter with the Love of our lives that is initiated by God Himself. *Prayer is the means whereby the Holy Spirit is afforded the opportunity to traverse through the corridors of our spirit, forming and transforming us so that we might experience the deepest possible dimensions of the life of God, and become perfected into the* imago Dei—*the image and likeness of God.* In other words, we become icons of Jesus in the world through the power of the Holy Spirit.

While it is true that during stormy episodes the practice of prayer is a challenging undertaking, Scripture encourages us to pray without ceasing even though the turbulence of attending events influence us to entertain the erroneous notion that our prayers are rising no higher than the rooftop. Scripture also tells us that the Holy Spirit prays on our behalf, transporting our concerns to Jesus who is seated at the right hand of God making intercession for us as our heavenly Mediator. In turn, the Spirit bears back to us all that Christ is. We have two intercessors praying fervently on our behalf at all times, enabling our prayers: the Spirit within us and Jesus the Son who is seated at the right hand of the Father. The Triune life of God flowing in and out of the three persons of the Godhead is the environment in which prayer takes place as the work of the three personalities flow into each other in an elegant choreography of divine love, working in a marvelous and mysterious dynamic that works on behalf of God's children.

God Desires We Pray Without Ceasing

Acquiring the deepest possible knowledge of the personality of God could only be accomplished by heeding Paul's admonition to pray without ceasing (see 1 Thess. 5:17). Even though God might not readily reveal His mysteries to us, we must remain open to the prospects of divine revelation by living with a sense of expectancy and maintaining a prayerful attitude at all times. While it is questionable as to whether or not we could live with our spiritual wicks turned up to such a height without burning out, we must trust God to provide us the stamina that makes Paul's admonition become a reality in our lives. And the means of realizing this transformative feat entails keeping our spiritual circuits attuned to what our heavenly Father might be saying to us.

Keeping our spirit attuned to God enables us to contemplate His glory, acquiring the deepest possible revelation of who He is. *We cannot worship that which we do not truly love.* The more disciplined our prayer life becomes, the more our being becomes saturated with the energy and power of prayer, because when we experience a deepened relationship with God, our lives become enriched and thereby affording the Creator the opportunity to impart the Holy Spirit to us in full measure. *When we allow God the opportunity to impart the Holy Spirit to us in full measure, we become conformed to His divine nature and engrafted to live fully from the true source of life.*

The spiritual climate of our lives at any given point in time is contingent on the source from which we live—that which we are connected to. Jesus's admonition that His disciples should "live" from Him because He is the True Vine was no idle exhortation. Our Lord is intimately aware of the fact that the forces to which we are connected and draw succor on a continuous basis ultimately determine the quality of our life experiences. This truth is corroborated by the words of Luke when he reminded believers of the reality that it is from the Holy Spirit that we live, move, and have our beings fixed (see Acts 17:28).

Not only does prayer allow God the opportunity to impart His nature to us in full measure, it also allows Him the opportunity to become acquainted with all aspects of our personality (see Ps. 139:1-6). Prayer also avails us power for the living of our days as we receive impartation from God, thereby allowing the very life of God to invade us, becoming operational within our lives. While God is intimately acquainted with every aspect of our existence, prayer creates the environment that enables us to voluntarily bare our soul to our heavenly Father. Unabashed prayer ushers us to the place where we recognize the need to dispense with pious platitudes, and grants our heavenly Father the opportunity to deal with us as we really are—sinners in need of transformation.

Baring of the soul presents God with the opportunity to transform those walled-off areas of our lives that we are prone to keep hidden in the shadows, fearful that He might not accept us. *God accepts us and stoops to meet us in whatever condition we might find ourselves.* However, before we can experience transformation in all aspects of our being, we need to take a page from David's playbook, acknowledge our sin, and ask God to create a new heart within us. The ability to ask God for a new heart signifies our arrival at the station in life where we recognize our need for divine help so we might experience transformation of our life situation. It signifies our arrival at the state of humility where we are prepared to put all of our cards on the table, which engenders an atmosphere of transparency that opens us up to a deeper understanding of God's mercy and compassion, thus revealing to us that our heavenly Father is more interested in transforming us than in punishing us.

When our life's objective becomes that of seeking to know God on the most intimate basis possible through the practice of prayer, we voluntarily swing wide the door of our spirit, cultivating the climate in which uninhibited communion with the Creator can take place. The quest to know God on the most intimate basis possible enables us to fully embrace the words of Jesus: *"But seek ye first the kingdom of God, and His righteousness; and all these things shall be added unto you"* (Matt. 6:33). When our heart's desire becomes that of allowing the reign of God to be manifested in our lives through the radicalizing Holy Spirit that presents God with unhindered access to transform us, episodes of adversity are viewed from an entirely new perspective. While life's trials will undoubtedly prove to be unsettling, acknowledging the supremacy of God over every facet of our existence enables us to refract painful experiences through the prism of the Spirit, where we recognize our lives as secure in the grasp of God's encompassing love, and that nothing in all creation could separate us from His love.

So instead of running around frantically without any inkling about the source to which we should turn in those instances when painful experiences knock on our life's door, threatening to rip them off their hinges, the Holy Spirit beckons us to prayerfully turn to God and recognize that He alone is our security, our sure foundation, our rock in a weary land, and our shelter in times of storm. We should live the days of our lives with the blessed assurance that we are secure in the Creator's care. Becoming awakened to the great truth that we are secure in the Creator's care is also made possible through the study of Scripture, which happens to be the next rung of the ladder we are exhorted to grab hold of as we migrate from the fiery trials to the realization of God's all-sufficiency.

Reflection Questions

1. What efforts are you engaged in that are designed to help you cultivate a disciplined prayer life?

2. What are some things that might be hindering you from praying as you should?

3. Is the cultivation of a disciplined prayer life high on your list of priorities?

CHAPTER NINE

Utilize Scripture As a Guide for Living During Difficult Times

The writer of Hebrews tells us that the word of God is a living entity (see Heb. 4:12). Instead of simply being a compilation of heart-warming stories and doctrinal statements, the writer indicates that the Bible is a place that presents us the opportunity to experience an encounter with God. Additionally, it is through the pages of the Bible that we are acquainted with the means by which God employs painful experiences to transform the lives of individuals that He utilizes as emissaries to inaugurate His will on earth.

Abraham was 75 years of age when God instructed him to take a leap of faith into the unknown and sever ties with his ancestral home of Ur of the Chaldees, and relocate to a land that would be revealed to him at a later date. God's directive to the ancient patriarch was:

Now the Lord had said unto Abram, Get thee out of thy country, and from thy kindred, and from thy father's house,

unto a land that I will shew thee: and I will make of thee
a great nation, and I will bless thee, and make thy name
great; and thou shalt be a blessing: and I will bless them
that bless thee, and curse him that curseth thee: and in thee
shall all families of the earth be blessed (Genesis 12:1-3).

At an advanced age, when he was comfortable and well settled, God instructed Abraham to uproot his family and venture far beyond the confines of his comfort zone. Scripture is silent on the probing thoughts that actually transpired in the mind and heart of Abraham and his beloved bride Sarah as they gathered their earthly possessions together in preparation for an adventurous and uncertain foray into surroundings that were hitherto unfamiliar to them. However, the biblical record is unmistakably clear concerning the patriarch's response: *"So Abram departed, as the Lord had spoken unto him"* (Gen. 12:4). And the writer of Hebrews stated, *"By faith Abraham obeyed when he was called to set out for a place that he was to receive as an inheritance; and he set out, not knowing where he was going"* (Heb. 11:8 NRSV).

Abraham responded to God's directive, departing his native country in the company of his wife Sarah and his nephew Lot (see Gen. 12:5). Not only did the Creator reveal the boundaries of the land that he and his descendants were destined to inherit (see Gen. 15:18), but He also promised the patriarch an heir that would ensue from his loins (see Gen. 15:4). The biblical narrative indicates that during the extended sojourn in the wilderness, Abraham and Sarah were repeatedly tested in the area of their faith as it pertained to the heir that was promised to them by God. But when it appeared that God's promise did not materialize according to the timetable of the impatient couple, they employed their own device to make it a reality in their lives.

Abraham was confronted with a twin dilemma of sorts. First, his wife was barren and, in certain parts of the ancient Middle East, bareness was viewed as a curse that robbed women of their sense of womanhood. In lieu of this reality, women who were unable to conceive children lived each day of their lives burdened with the stigma of their infertility. Such was Sarah's plight. Secondly, Abraham was concerned that the genealogical line, stretching all the way back from the ancient prophet Shem (see Gen. 7:13) down to himself, would come to an abrupt end. And his existence would be erased from the historical record if Sarah was unable to birth babies of her own.

It was the accepted custom in certain regions of the ancient Middle East to utilize the mistress's handmaid as a surrogate mother to birth babies in those particular instances when the wife of the head of a household was unable to birth babies of her own. In light of her painful dilemma, Sarah invoked the ancient cultural prerogative, and availed her Egyptian handmaid Hagar as a surrogate wife to Abraham so that he might impregnate her and produce the promised heir (see Gen. 16:2-4).

To the couple's delight, the venture at impregnation was successful. But the offspring ensuing from the union between Abraham and Hagar failed to promote harmonious relations in the patriarch's household. Instead, it merely served to muddy the domestic waters. When Hagar realized that she was pregnant, she became puffed up and behaved in a disrespectful manner toward her barren mistress. And as time progressed, however, the relationship between the two women became so acrimonious that Sarah refused to put up with the smug and condescending behavior of her impudent rival. Determined to stake her claim as first lady in the patriarchal household and restore an atmosphere of civility around the family circle, Sarah treated Hagar harshly, prompting her to temporarily flee the desert compound (see Gen. 16:6).

Scripture indicates that Abraham was 84 years old when Hagar gave birth to Ishmael (see Gen. 16:16). Just six years later, at the ripe old age of 90, he was still fatherless with his beautiful and beloved bride (see Gen. 17:1). After 15 years of patiently waiting on God to manifest His promise in their lives, Abraham and his bride began to waver in their faith. At this juncture in time, God reaffirmed His promise of a son to the aged couple (see Gen. 17:19). From a physiological point of view, it was highly unlikely that Sarah would ever give birth to a baby at her advanced age. In lieu of the biological improbability, Abraham found it difficult to wrap his mind around the fact that God's promise would materialize at such an advanced stage of their lives, prompting him to commiserate to the Creator over the possibility of Ishmael becoming his heir (see Gen. 17:18). In response to Abraham's impatience, God provided him with the name of the son that Sarah was destined to birth at a future date (see Gen. 17:19).

At the advanced age of 99, just nine years subsequent to the date that God provided Abraham with the name Isaac (*yizaq* in Hebrew), divine messengers materialized at his desert compound while he sat in his tent door attempting to shade himself from the blazing desert sun. The three mysterious emissaries informed Abraham that within the space of a year Sarah would give birth to a son (see Gen. 17:18-19). When Sarah overheard the men informing the old man that she was destined to become a mother, she was amused by the absurdity of the prophetic declaration, and laughed uproariously while simultaneously questioning her ability to produce offspring at such an advanced age in her life.

The messengers were incensed over Sarah's unbelief and questioned Abraham as to why his bride found the divine announcement to be amusing. One of the messengers further inquired: *"Is anything too hard for the Lord?"* (Gen. 18:14). Remaining true to His promise, God blessed Sarah, and she gave birth to a baby boy one year later when Abraham had attained the advanced age of 100 (see Gen. 21:5).

Abraham and Sarah had been put through the wringer, so to speak. Twenty-five years were rolled into eternity from the time that God disclosed His covenant promise to the couple until the miraculous event of Sarah actually birthing a son, thereby signifying that God's delays are in no way God's denials. On several occasions during the long wait, the impatient couple became frustrated over their inability to produce offspring of their own. On account of this reality, the stress of the relationship became so intolerable at times that it subjected them to an acrimonious and emotional roller-coaster ride. But despite the tumultuous interim during which they were required to wait on God's providence, the Almighty demonstrated that the fulfillment of the promised event was entirely contingent on His ability to send the answer when—and only when—the time was right. The fulfillment of the promised event was contingent on His divine timing—His *kairos*. While the impatient couple were fixated on physiology as it pertained to God's promise materializing in their lives, God demonstrated that His promises are in no way constrained by physiology or other phenomena, because He is the Almighty One—*Jehovah El Shaddai*—and nothing is too hard for the Creator.

Another biblical personality who was compelled to wait an inordinate amount of time before experiencing transformation of his life situation is Moses. After being rescued from the river

Nile by the Pharaoh's daughter (see Exod. 2:6), Moses lived at the pinnacle of prestige and privilege as a powerful prince of Egypt. Unfortunately, he fell out of favor with the ruling Pharaoh when he took matters into his own hands, killing one of the taskmasters the king had assigned over the enslaved Hebrew nation residing in the territory of Goshen, in Egypt's Delta region. After killing the taskmaster, Moses disposed of the corpse in a shallow grave, which he hurriedly dug in the warm Egyptian sand. When Pharaoh got wind of Moses's action, he sought retribution against the rebellious prince in order to kill him. To preserve his life, Moses fled Egypt, crossing the border into the land of Midian, where he secured safe sanctuary and employment as a shepherd caring for the flock of Jethro, priest of Midian. He subsequently married Jethro's daughter, Zipporah, and the union between the couple produced a son whom they named Gershom.

Moses spent solitary nights under the canopy of the starstudded sky in the cool, windswept Midian desert, where he was given ample time to reflect on his former life of leisure as a powerful prince in the opulence of Pharaoh's palace. On numerous occasions, while daydreaming or watching the twinkling stars dance across the bejeweled desert sky, he undoubtedly questioned the wisdom of attempting to balance the scales of injustice when he took matters into his own hands to prevent the slain taskmaster from registering additional blows to the person of his Hebrew brother—it was another Hebrew brother who witnessed what transpired and betrayed his murderous actions to Pharaoh. In retrospect, he probably wished he had minded his own business, because he might very well have attained the status of Pharaoh at some future date. But this was all water under the bridge at the present time. After 40 years out in the wilderness, when no change appeared to be registering on the radar screen of his advancing life, the fugitive prince undoubtedly resigned himself to the prospects of spending the remaining years of his uneventful existence as a common shepherd out in the windswept desert. Unexpectedly, at the age of 80, God showed up on the doorstep of Moses's life and commenced writing a new and fascinating chapter that altered the trajectory of human history.

Scripture informs us that Moses was tending sheep out in the wilderness when an angel of the Lord appeared to him in the midst of a burning bush. And by some miraculous means, the bush was not consumed by the fire engulfing it. God identified Himself to Moses as I AM out of the burning bush, issuing him the divine assignment as liberator of the Hebrew nation that was currently enslaved in Egypt (see Exod. 1:7-14). Not only did Moses subsequently confront Pharaoh, but he also orchestrated the emancipation of the Hebrew nation from Egyptian bondage by means of punishing plagues that were unleashed against the Egyptians. By divine providence, he became the lawgiver to whom God provided the Ten Commandments to humankind on Mount Sinai (see Exod. 20). And each of the three major religions—Christianity, Islam, and Judaism—recognize Moses as one of the patriarchs of their ancient religious tradition.

Before relinquishing leadership of the emancipated Hebrew congregation that he frequently referred to in moments of utter frustration as a "stiff-necked people," Moses was tested in every conceivable way possible. Little did he realize that God would employ his 40-year season of desert isolation as the laboratory in which to prepare him for the assignment as liberator and lawgiver of the enslaved Hebrew nation. After being compelled to accept the unsolicited portfolio, God utilized Moses's repertoire of experiences as events to teach him the important lessons of humility, patience, faith, hope, and the need to rely exclusively on the providence of Jehovah God. Scripture indicates that Moses cultivated a personal relationship with God and spoke to the Creator *"face to face, as one speaks to a friend"* (Exod. 33:11 NRSV). Both Abraham and Moses came to know God in the most intimate of ways, enabling the Creator to employ the trials to which they were subjected as the means whereby He would prepare them for utilization as instruments to inaugurate His divine plan on earth.

While Scripture provides us with information as to how God employed difficult experiences to fashion individuals into instruments that were utilized to orchestrate His divine plan on earth, the life lessons of Abraham and Moses additionally illustrate that Scripture is a means whereby God's children are able to unite with His wisdom, align their lives with His commandments, and engage in concrete steps that serve to promote unity with the Divine. In other words, Scripture it is a means whereby humankind receive knowledge as to how we might approximate the *imago Dei*— the image and likeness of God.

Both Abraham and Moses found themselves between a rock and a hard place. First, Abraham was instructed to relinquish the security of his ancestral home and relocate to a far away and foreign land. He was asked to engage in the unthinkable and culturally frowned upon act of severing long-established ancestral bonds and venture into an uncertain future. Secondly, Moses had an assignment that was placed on him that he really had no stomach for. If the truth be told, he undoubtedly entertained no inclination of ever returning to his former home where he would be compelled to face the music of the Egyptian criminal justice system. He was painfully aware of the fact that he was a fugitive felon. If given the option to choose, he probably would have chosen to remain in the sanctuary of the Midian wilderness with his beloved family. However, despite the consternation of both men as it pertained to their particulars of their individual situations, God had bigger plans for them. But without faith in the Almighty, they would have been unable to respond to the divine directive and experience transformation in their life situation.

When the names of Abraham and Moses are invoked, we immediately conjure up larger-than-life characters. But such was not always the case. Both individuals were initially resistant to the call of God on their lives as many modern-day pilgrims are. But, by responding to God's call, not only was the Creator able to utilize Abraham and Moses as instruments to inaugurate His divine plan on earth, He was also afforded the opportunity to transform their lives despite the initial resistance to His call.

Like Abraham and Moses, God is not merely desirous that we respond to His directive; His primary objective is the transformation of our life situation. God does not simply want us to respond to His call on our lives, He is desirous that we submit the nerve center of our consent to His sovereignty in order that His desire might become our desire. He wants His Spirit to become one with our spirit, evidenced by the words of Jesus when He declared that He and His Father are one (see John 17:11). Our heavenly Father wants to fashion us into the *imago Dei*—the image and likeness of God. He wants to fashion us into icons of God on planet earth. And He wants to claim us for Himself. This is what the salvation story is all about. And it is by surrendering our entire being to the sovereignty of God that we become transformed into His image and likeness.

In addition to learning from Scripture how God inaugurates His divine plan in the universe and transforms the lives of individuals that are utilized to inaugurate His divine plan in the universe, Scripture is also the means whereby we acquire knowledge concerning the personality of God. We would never be able to respond to the call of God on our lives if we are oblivious to those instances when He is speaking to us. And we would never be able to love and worship God until we can become intimately acquainted with the personality of God. Additionally, we will never be able to become acquainted with the personality of God if God does not reveal Himself to us. It is imperative that we learn through Scripture the means whereby we might respond to God's initiatives to communicate with us.

Before God could ever reveal Himself to us, there must be a willingness on our part to open ourselves up to divine revelation. Since God cannot be conjured up on our terms and under the conditions of our choosing, we must avail ourselves to the path whereby He is able to disclose Himself to us, and one such means is by investing adequate time in the study of Scripture. By meditating on Scripture, we purpose the tributaries of our spirit to the invasive rush of the Holy Spirit where God's life enlivens us and takes possession of us. By taking possession of our spirit, the Holy Spirit graces us with the mind of Christ, giving Him the opportunity to guide our responses to life. Since we can never will God to reveal Himself to us, it is through faith that we open ourselves up to knowing God in the most intimate way possible, because God avails us grace that enables us to enter into a loving relationship with divine love.

Meditating on Scripture does not necessarily mean that we should read God's word in a casual manner as we read an ordinary book. Peter Toon writes in *The Art of Meditating on Scripture* that the sacred text should be read slowly, prayerfully, and formatively—and preferably aloud. The author makes a distinction between informative reading and formative reading. He indicates that informative reading is undertaken in the way someone reads a letter, newspaper, or book, and it is a means of acquiring information. On the other hand, formative reading is done in a way that allows the sacred text to form us—to give the Holy Spirit opportunity to be in charge, allowing the inspirer of Scripture to become for us its illustrator so that its content (a little at a time) enters our soul.[1] The action of God's word in our lives transforms our hearts in order that God's love is manifested in a palpable way, thereby demonstrating our love for the Creator.

During Paul's second missionary journey, he was jailed in Philippi and experienced a near riot in Thessalonica. During the challenging and angst-ridden period in the great apostle's life, he and his companions were subjected to the hospitality of the Bereans. Luke writes: *"These* [Bereans] *were more noble than those in Thessalonica, in that they received the word with all readiness of mind, and searched the scriptures daily, whether those things were so"* (Acts 17:11). The Bereans were elated about the good news of salvation that they received from Paul and his disciples. The enthusiastic reception of God's word on the part of the citizens of Berea served to immortalize them in the annals of biblical history.

Enthusiasm concerning the study of God's word is a concrete demonstration of the transformative action wrought by the word of God in our own lives. Jesus declared: *"Those who **love** Me will keep My word, and My Father will love them, and We will come to them and make Our home with them"* (John 14:23 NRSV). The majestic Creator of the universe is a friend who tabernacles with us in every facet of our life situation. Because of this, we ought to be enthusiastic about God's presence and the life-transforming words that He avails us through the study of Scripture. We must recognize God's words as sacraments that minister to us in our mountaintop experiences as well as during the dark and despairing valleys of life's difficult circumstances. But more importantly, Scripture is a means of providing us with encounters with God that serve to transform our lives and sustain us through the most difficult of life's experiences. A demonstration of God's power to cradle us in His protective care is what we will now look at in the final chapter of this book.

Reflection Questions

1. Do you approach Bible reading with the expectancy that God has a specific message for you in the biblical text?

2. Do you make a deliberate and informed resolution to change an attitude or behavior in light of having read some biblical passage?

3. Do you approach Bible reading with the intent of not only seeking revelation of who God is, but also what He is calling you to be?

CHAPTER TEN

God Did It

Tragedy Strikes

From a vantage point well into the second half of her life, and armed with a fortress-like faith in Almighty God, Kay considers herself to be a walking miracle. Born of African-American descent into a working class family in Columbia, South Carolina, Kay is intimately aware of the dark side of Jim Crow racial segregation that once plagued the American South. Her subjection to second-class citizenry in her native land compelled her to develop an inner toughness that enabled her to cope with the jagged realities of her proscribed status.

After graduating from high school, Kay relocated to New York City to secure an economically better future and escape the absurdities with which she was compelled to live in the racially segregated South. At this juncture in her life, she embraced the assumption that she was adequately equipped to confront the very worst that life could ever hurl at her. This belief imploded at a later date in life when she was plunged into incomprehensible suffering ensuing from the death of her two beloved sons, Tony and Eric.

After relocating to New York City, she settled in the borough of the Bronx, working at odd jobs to secure the necessary funds that enabled her to pay her way through night school, where she pursued a course in secretarial studies. After completing her studies, she sat for the New York State exam to become a stenographer, which she passed with flying colors. She began her employment with the Department of Motor Vehicles, and later worked for several other state agencies before retiring with more than 30 years of service.

Shortly after relocating to New York, Kay met her husband, Augusta, affectionately referred to by family and friends as Gus. He worked in the printing business. The couple raised three rambunctious boys—Tony, Eric, and Alvin—providing them with a loving home environment where they showered them with love and affection, and gave them a solid educational foundation. Both parents taught their sons to love and respect themselves and their neighbors. Above all else, they taught them to fear God. Despite the occasional round of youthful indiscretions which parents are subjected to when children occasionally get out of line, Kay and Gus were pleased with the way the three boys eventually turned out.

By the time they were teenagers, they were well-adjusted individuals who were gainfully employed in their unique occupational pursuits. Recognizing that her sons had finally grown up, Kay believed that she had crossed the biggest hurdle of her life. Having successfully raised three African-American young men belonging to a segment of society that is encumbered by seemingly insurmountable problems gave her a sense of accomplishment. Kay subscribed to the tenet of the African-American abolitionist and former slave Frederick Douglas, who believed that it is better to raise strong sons than to repair broken men. Just when she thought that it was smooth sailing, tragedy knocked on her door, threatening to unravel her to the core.

After what initially appeared to be nothing more than routine flu-like symptoms, Kay's eldest son, Tony, began experiencing respiratory problems that persisted for an unusual length of time. After consulting with doctors at a local hospital, Tony was diagnosed with lung cancer. The prognosis took the wind out of the sails of family members in lieu of the fact that Tony never smoked or consumed alcoholic beverages. The diagnosis was a baffling and troubling pronouncement. He remained in the hospital where he underwent a regimen of chemotherapy. Unfortunately, the chemotherapy did not halt the march of the disease from taking over his body or cause it to go into remission. His was a hopeless case.

In a similar manner to the physicians who treated the woman who was afflicted with the issue of blood, the physician assigned to Tony's case concluded that there was nothing more he could do for him, and simply sent him home to die. Terrified at the prospects confronting him, Tony questioned the physician, "Doctor, are you sending me home to die?" When no answer was forthcoming from the physician, Tony turned to his mother and implored, "Mom, do something, please. I am too young to die. I can't die yet. I've never been sick Momma, so why am I going through this?" He continued, "I don't drink or smoke or take drugs like some guys, and I've never been sick, so why am I going through this Momma?"

Unable to locate adequate words which she might employ to assuage her son's anxieties, Kay responded to his questions the best way she knew how, telling him, "Tony, God has the last say.

You are His child, and He loves you; so let's trust Him." The reality of her son's impending demise was simply too much for her to bear. It hit her like a ton of bricks, causing her to experience angst that tore at the very core of her being. She, however, recognized that she needed to remain strong for her Tony, especially since he recognized that she had a deep and abiding relationship with God, and that she was for all practical purposes his spiritual bulwark.

After Tony was discharged from the hospital when no help was forthcoming from the medical staff, Kay and Gus refurbished the basement of their family home, installing a hospital bed, oxygen and intercom systems, and other essential medical equipment that would make Tony's final days on earth as comfortable as possible. After being reduced to a state of utter dependence on his mother and other family members, Tony seized every available opportunity to express his deep appreciation to his mother for her kind and compassionate care as she ministered to his every need, telling her, "Mom, I'm so sorry to put you through this."

Kay would simply reply, "Tony, I am sure that you would do the same thing for me."

Late one evening, Tony summoned his mother on the intercom system, requesting that she proceed down into the basement where he was staying. When Kay arrived at Tony's bedside, he informed her that he saw Jesus in a dream. Kay inquired as to what He looked like. Tony responded telling her that he did not actually see the Master's face. He proceeded however to tell her that in the dream he was in a room, and someone kept encouraging him to proceed into an adjoining room. However, he finally overcame his reluctance and entered the room. He said that when he entered the room, Jesus was there and everything was beautiful.

After listening to the details of Tony's dream, Kay began leaping with excitement and praising God. She saw the dream as validation that Jesus was aware of her son's predicament, and that He had prepared a room for him as promised in the Bible (see John 14:1-3). Kay disclosed to Tony that his dream was the most beautiful testimony that she had ever heard in her life. In the ensuing days, Tony eventually came to grips with the reality that his days on earth were numbered. However, he still held out hope that Jesus would one day provide him with answers as to why he had to endure so much pain and suffering at such an early stage in his life. But the answers never came.

Even though Tony was confronted with adversity of the worst kind, he was still concerned about the financial burdens that his sickness subjected his family to. Not wanting to burden them with financial problems, he inquired as to whether or not they had adequate funds on hand to pay for his medical and funeral expenses. He also inquired as to whether or not family members residing in South Carolina would make the long trip up to New York to pay their last respects to him at his home-going service. Kay informed him not to worry about such trivial matters, because she and Gus had adequate savings on hand to provide him with the best funeral possible. She additionally informed him that family members from South Carolina would most certainly travel to New York to attend his funeral.

A few nights before Tony made his initiation into eternity, Gus suggested to Kay that they should stay in the basement with him. On the night in question, the home attendant who provided round-the-clock care for Tony indicated that he was having difficulty breathing. After experiencing a great deal of respiratory distress, Tony prevailed upon his parents to take him to the emergency room (ER) at the hospital as quickly as possible where the medical staff could better address his situation. After arriving at the ER and being admitted to the hospital, Tony observed several physicians congregating in close proximity to his bed. They in hushed tones, and occasionally throwing glances in his direction. Noticing their actions, Tony exclaimed to his father, "They know I'm dying."

A short while after Tony made the comment to his father, he requested that Kay steady his writing hand with her own hand so that he might sign the medical directive that prevented them from resuscitating him in the event that he went into cardiac arrest. After signing the directive commonly known as a Do Not Resuscitate (DNR) request, which was Tony's desire, one of the physicians administered pain medication that enabled him to get some much-needed sleep. But even during sleep, his breathing continued to be labored. After several hours in the emergency room, Kay and Gus returned home to get themselves a few hours of much-needed sleep.

The following morning, which was Saturday, Kay and Gus returned to the hospital. On this second visit, Kay's sister accompanied them. At this point in time, Tony had been transferred to the hospital ward. He was awake when his family members arrived, and he kept repeating how much he loved them, and wanted them to promise him that they would continue to care for his two-year-old son, Deonte. Each individual concerned promised Tony that they would do everything in their power to make absolutely sure that his young son received the best care possible until such time that he was old enough to care for himself. Tony went home to glory to be with his Lord the following day, Sunday. He was 30 years old.

On the occasion of Kay's last visit to the hospital, two evangelists from her church accompanied her. The three of them left immediately after the Sunday service was over. One of the evangelists
is a registered nurse at one of the area hospitals. When Kay and
her colleagues arrived at the hospital, they discovered Alvin, Kay's
second son, sitting at Tony's bedside. Alvin indicated that since his
arrival at the hospital Tony had been asleep. After being informed
that Kay was on site, the attending physician informed Kay that
the medical staff was administering morphine to Tony as a palliative for his pain to keep him as comfortable as possible.

After a short while, Alvin indicated that he was returning
home to give Kay and her church brethren time to be alone with
Tony. After Alvin left, Kay took Tony's hand into her own and
began whispering tenderly in his ear, repeatedly telling him how
much she loved him. She additionally informed him that she had
brought a few members of her church to minister to him. Kay recalled that at an earlier point during his illness, Tony had indicated his desire of one day being able to return to church where he
could worship God in the sanctuary with other believers. During
the visit, one of the evangelists read selected passages of Scripture
even though they recognized that Tony might not have been
aware of the readings. After Scripture was read, everyone sung the
hymn, "When We All Get to Heaven."

Shortly after the conclusion of scripture reading and singing,
the nurse assigned to care for Tony entered his room and took his
vital signs. Then the nurse hurried out of the room with a worried
look framing her face. She returned shortly thereafter with the attending physician in tow. The physician examined Tony, and then
asked to speak privately with Kay outside of the room. When Kay

and the physician were out of earshot of the individuals remaining in the room, the physician said to Kay, "You do know that your son is dying, don't you?" Kay responded to the question, asking him how much time he thought Tony had left to live. The physician replied, "A few hours."

At the conclusion of the conversation with the physician, Kay returned to the room, where she rejoined her church sisters in singing hymns. A few minutes after Kay reentered the room, one of the evangelists whispered silently into her ear, "Kay, the angels are here, they're here, and they've come for Tony." Within a few short minutes after the prophetic announcement, Tony stopped breathing. Kay let go of her son's hand which she was holding at the time, walked out of the room, and informed the nursing staff that God had taken her son home to glory.

When he was notified about Tony's passing, the attending physician returned to the room and officially pronounced him dead. Shortly thereafter, several members of the hospital staff stopped by the room to offer their condolences to Kay and her family, indicating how sorry they were about her loss.

A member of the nursing staff disclosed to Kay that she was a believer in Jesus, and the Christian witness that she demonstrated on the occasions when she visited with her son served as a powerful testimony to her members of the hospital staff. The nurse indicated that Kay's testimony had personally inspired her to remain steadfast in her allegiance to Christ. After receiving the kind words from the appreciative nurse, Kay responded by expressing her heartfelt thanks to members of the hospital staff for the exceptional care that was dispensed to her son during his stay in the institution. She then made her way back to the dearly departed's beside, where she grabbed hold of his cold and lifeless hand and caressed it one last time. Overcome by the numbing flood of emotions that rolled over and through her body, Kay slowly turned around and began walking through the dark valley that stretched out endlessly before her. It suddenly dawned on her that her darling son had left her forever. Forever? Such a thought was simply too much to bear. As she made her way out of the hospital, the warm and salty tears flowed down her cheeks in an endless flood.

Tony's home-going service was presided over by Kay's pastor at her church. The sanctuary was filled with family members from South Carolina who made the trip up to New York City to pay their last respects to their beloved cousin. In addition to family members from the South and the local area, friends of Tony and individuals who might not have known him personally but knew his family showed up to pay their final respects. Sitting in the front row of the church, in close proximity to Tony's casket, which was lying in front of the pulpit, Kay was of the opinion that Tony was somehow pleased with the magnificent send off that was accorded him.

In the weeks following Tony's funeral, family and friends no longer called or visited Kay as frequently as they did immediately after the death of her son. The sense of being alone proved to be a tremendous challenge for her. She walked around in a daze like a zombie, feeling empty on the inside, needing to talk to anyone who would listen to her. The fact that she arrived home from work on or about 4 P.M., and her husband, Gus, and her youngest son, Eric, did not arrive home until on or about 7 P.M., exacerbated her situation. Feelings of loneliness gnawed at her insides as the days progressed to the point that she no longer had the desire to come home to an empty house.

In an attempt to have some companionship before her family members arrived home, Kay frequently met with a friend at a restaurant in close proximity to her home, where they shared meals and passed the hours in conversation. On those occasions when she did not meet with her friend, Kay would bring the family dog, Ace, into the house from the backyard where he was kept. She utilized Ace as a companion to occupy the hours that her friend usually filled, running with him up and down the stairs from the basement, shouting and praising God. Unfortunately, Ace became terminally ill and had to be euthanized. Kay was subjected to another loss.

After losing Ace, Kay's sense of loneliness magnified. She refused to allow the hurt that she experienced deep on the inside to imprison her in a house of pain, and decided to do something about her plight. After arriving home from work on the day of her resolution, she proceeded down into the basement of the family home, got down on her knees, and began pouring her heart out to God. She lamented over and over again: "Lord, You said that no weapon formed against me shall prosper. Take this pain, I can't handle it. It is too much, Lord." After an extended period of unburdening herself at the foot of the cross, Kay felt a warm sensation moving through her body.

During her period of lament she was lying prostrate on the couch which she usually utilized as her altar. She then rolled over and fell to the floor where she lay prostrate for an unknown period of time. Recognizing that a change had come over her, she excitedly exclaimed, "Lord, just look at You; look at what You've done." She was so overwhelmed by the sense of relief that permeated every fiber of her being that she began laughing so hard she could not stop herself. Kay realized that the feeling she was experiencing was undoubtedly what the Bible referred to as the *"peace of God, which surpasses all understanding"* (Phil. 4:7 NRSV). Miraculously, her joy for living had returned.

Another Tragedy

Ten years after Tony's death, Kay and her family were in the process of making preparations to attend a family reunion in her native South Carolina. Members of her deceased mother's side of the family sponsored the reunion, and everyone was excited about rekindling family relationships. The event was scheduled for the weekend of August 14th of the same year.

On the morning of August 8th, Kay and Gus became concerned when their youngest son Eric did not come home the previous night. This was uncharacteristic behavior for him. Kay's sister-in-law and her family were visiting from California at the time, and Kay knew that Eric would certainly want to spend as much time as he possibly could with them. Because of this, she was confused over the behavior of her then 33-year-old son, prompting her to filter events of the past days through her memory bank to see if she could pinpoint anything unusual about Eric's behavior. During the process of reflection, Kay recalled that on the previous evening of August 6th, she was looking at a television program in the living room and later dozed off. After waking up from nodding off, she observed Eric sitting across from her in a chair. She could see the light from the television set reflecting in his eyes, and she surmised that he was staring at her. She questioned Eric as to why he was staring at her, and he simply denied that he was doing any such thing. The scenario played itself out on two subsequent occasions during the night. She also remembered that for some odd reason Eric kept looking at the clock. A few hours after she had nodded off for a second time, Eric woke her up and informed her that he was going out.

Eric did not return home until 5 P.M. on the following day, August 7th. When he arrived home, his aunt questioned him about his whereabouts. He informed her that he had spent the hours away from home walking around the borough. Kay was aware of the fact that her son frequently took long walks around the neighborhood, but his behavior at this point in time was highly unusual. She told him at that point that if something was on his mind that compelled him to walk around the borough for almost an entire day, that it might be helpful for him to consult with a physician. During the conversation with Eric, Kay observed that both of his eyes were extremely swollen and bloodshot. She questioned him as to whether or not he had been crying. But he never responded to the question. He simply observed himself in the mirror, and indicated that he was going out to the corner store to buy himself another pack of cigarettes.

Eric had a close relationship with his older brother, Tony. He loved the very earth on which Tony walked, and never really appeared to come to grips with his brother's death. At no time since Tony's death did he ever talk to friends or family members concerning thoughts of their time together, leading many to conclude that he never really experienced closure over his sibling's death. The suspicions of family members and friends eventually rang true. As time ensued, Eric began suffering from bouts of depression, necessitating that he be admitted to a hospital where he received psychiatric treatment for his illness. From the time of the initial treatment session, he continued to receive injections every 30 days in order to help him cope with his illness.

Eric did not return home on August 7th after indicating that he was going out once more to buy another pack of cigarettes at the corner store. Perturbed over her son's behavior, Kay sat in the living room pondering his whereabouts. Unexpectedly, the front doorbell rang, jolting her out of her deep thoughts. She knew that Eric did not ring the bell because he had keys to the front door. Besides, there would be no reason for him to ring the doorbell. Kay opened the door and observed two unfamiliar and unsmiling men standing on her doorstep. Their professional demeanor of the individuals suggested that they were on a special assignment.

One of the individuals inquired about Kay's identity, and wanted to know if she had a son by the name of Eric. Overcome by a daunting sense of unease, Kay instinctively blurted out, "Where is my son? Where is my baby?"

One of the men responded to her inquiry, stating, "Lady, I'm sorry, your son is dead." The men identified themselves as detectives from the investigative unit of the New York City Police Department (NYPD), and proceeded to inform Kay that Eric jumped to his death from the University Heights Bridge into the swirling waters of the Harlem River below. The University Heights Bridge separates the Inwood section of the Bronx from Manhattan Island as New York City is known.

Overcome by unimaginable grief in whose vice-like grip she found herself, Kay began screaming, "No, Eric, don't do it. Don't do it." Traumatized by the dreadful news, Kay collapsed onto the floor in a state of hysteria and blacked out.

Eric's home-going service took place on the evening of Wednesday, August 13th, and his burial took place the following day on August 14th. It was déjà vu all over again. Kay had been through the fire ten years earlier, and the second round of adversity did not make her current ordeal any easier to handle. Anxiety over her predicament raced through her mind, threatening to drive her over the edge into a state of mental derangement. A few hours after Eric's internment at a local cemetery, Kay and several family members departed for South Carolina to participate in the already planned family reunion. Gus believed that it would be beneficial for everyone concerned to get away for a little respite and put some needed distance between the painful events of the past week. Kay was in total agreement with her husband's suggestion, and took the long trip back to her roots in South Carolina.

Kay and her family members returned to New York on August 17th. In the ensuing days, she felt as though she would suffocate under the burden of grief that assaulted her on a daily basis. She recalled that at no time in the past was any family member separated from each other for more than a two-week stretch, except on the occasion when Tony was hospitalized. While Tony's departure from the family circle proved to be an awful blow, Eric's departure compounded and complicated matters. It was simply staggering.

Kay was now retired from decades of employment with New York State. As such, she was home alone from 4 A.M., when her husband left for work in the printing business, until he returned home later in the evenings at about seven. In order to initiate contact with other individuals, she got out of bed about 5 A.M. and sat on her front steps watching people pass by on their daily pursuits. When sitting on her front steps no longer appeased her feelings of loneliness, Kay would get into her car and drive aimlessly around the Bronx with no particular destination in mind. Little did she realize that she oftentimes drove at such extremely low rates of speed that she threatened to bring traffic to a standstill. The occurrence of a frightening and potentially deadly event brought this reality home to her, and scared her out of her wits.

Kay disclosed that on the eventful morning when she was scared out of her wits, she was involved in one of her customary drives along a major thoroughfare in the Bronx, when an irate driver behind her began honking his automobile horn, requesting that she get out of the way and allow him to overtake her. Being preoccupied with thoughts of her deceased son, she was oblivious to the incessant honking, until she recognized hearing what appeared to be gunshots going off. She suddenly realized that the irate driver was shooting at her car. Fortunately, none of the bullets found their mark on her vehicle, leaving her to believe that the individual concerned merely wanted to scare her. Yet again, he might simply have been a poor marksman. Kay was scared and angry. She was traumatized over the fact that she could have been senselessly killed in a hail of gunfire. And she was angry for being immersed in a requiem of grief for having lost another son. Her sense of grief caused her to resonate with Job's predicament when he was suddenly bereft of his ten beloved children.

Every morning Kay got out of bed after Gus departed for work and engaged in private devotions. During early morning devotions, she played gospel music, listened to sermons, and engaged in praise and worship to God. On these occasions she made it a point of reminding God how huge her trial was. On one occasion she became so overwhelmed by the adversity assaulting her being that she disclosed to God, "Lord, if You wanted to hit me with a big one, this is it." She frequently retreated to Eric's room and engaged in devotions at that location. She frequently remained at that location for the entire day, where Gus found her when he returned home from work later in the evening.

Burdened by grief that sapped her vitality, Kay at one point disclosed to Gus that she did not know if she was going to survive her current ordeal. Recognizing that his bride was having a tough spell bearing her cross, Gus advised her to stay out of Eric's room. On one occasion he became so frustrated with her refusal to heed his advice that he intimated that if she did not pull herself together, Eric would come back for her. Kay recognized that Gus's stern demeanor bode no ill feelings toward her, and she simply promised to change her behavior. However, coping was difficult because she had difficulty falling asleep, and she frequently lost her appetite. Kay recognized that she was the prime candidate for a complete nervous breakdown.

After the gunshot incident, Kay discontinued her driving excursions around the Bronx. However, she would still sit on her doorstep or stand at her front window and watch people go by. On occasion, a young man bearing striking physical characteristics to those of Eric would pass by and capture her attention. She would stare at the young man until he disappeared from view, leaving her to ponder what he would have looked like had he lived.

Living Life With Broken Things

Kay's life was irreparably broken—at least certain aspects of it were. The landscape of her existence had been irrevocably altered, and there were certain things that could not be fixed or replaced— her two beloved sons would never return to her, and this painful pill was a difficult one for her to swallow.

The reality of Kay's brokenness hit home in a palpable way one Saturday morning while she lay in bed reflecting on her difficult life situation. She was painfully aware of the fact that family and friends were deeply concerned about her welfare, evidenced by the fact that Gus admonished her to stay out of Eric's room.

She knew that he meant well, and was merely trying as best as he knew how to pull her out of the doldrums. As she reflected on her painful sojourn up life's road, she somehow felt a sense of gratitude and began praising God for providing her with the strength to endure the hardships assaulting her being.

As she continued to praise God, the thought surfaced in her spirit that even though she was broken, she was certainly not beaten. Armed with the liberating and life-changing insight, she decided that she would make a concerted effort with God's grace to "pull herself together," just as Gus had recommended. She realized that even though God did not change her circumstances, He could change her.

Kay had entrusted her life to Christ since her youth. However, she realized that she needed to know God in the most intimate way possible. As she lay in bed on the eventful Saturday morning reflecting on her life's trajectory, the Holy Spirit brought to her memory the fact that several years ago a friend had provided her with information concerning evening classes at one of the local seminaries. She later contacted the institution during business hours to inquire about available programs. One week later Kay was enrolled in the institution's Certificate Program and had begun taking classes.

Religious studies proved to be an exciting and stimulating undertaking that Kay enjoyed immensely. She eagerly anticipated attendance at each class session, in addition to enjoying fellowship with kindred spirits on the path that she now found herself. Everything appeared to be going well until tragedy struck again. Four months after enrolling in seminary, Kay felt a lump in one of her breasts, and after consulting with a physician, she was diagnosed with breast cancer. She concluded at this point in time that in no way was she going back into the dark cave of depression from which she had recently emerged, and that she would trust God to bear her burden. She reminded God that Scripture indicated that *"the government shall be upon **His** shoulder"* (Isa. 9:6). As such, she entrusted the government of her life situation to Jesus—the One capable of bearing her burden.

After enduring months of treatment for cancerous lesions in her breast, Kay was subjected to a mammogram, only to be told after the procedure that she now had another type of malignancy in the other breast. Refusing to surrender to the painful diagnosis, she cried out like Job, "Lord, even though You might slay me, yet will I trust You" (see Job 13:15). Kay's trust in God's providential care served her well as He held her close in a comforting and peaceful embrace. With God's help, and the clinical expertise of skilled physicians, the cancerous lesions were successfully removed from both of Kay's breasts, thereby enabling her to continue in her studies at the seminary. Kay graduated from the Certificate Program two years later.

Living the Way of the Cross

Looking back over the arc of her tumultuous experiences, Kay recognized that her survival was wholly contingent on the providential care of what Francis Schaeffer described as "the God who is there."[1] She recognized that God, in a mysterious way, brings us new life through death. In theological terms, this is the "paschal mystery" that resides at the very heart of the Christian faith.

As Kay reflected on her painful experience, the words of Jesus were indelibly inscribed on the tapestry of her spirit, reminding her that if she was desirous of following Him, she would be compelled to take up her cross and follow Him (see Matt. 16:24). Recognizing that her season of cross-bearing was is no way alien to the Christian journey, Kay cultivated a deep relationship with God that enabled her to grow in grace and mature in her spiritual formation.

Spiritual writer David G. Benner informs us that the way of the Cross is not marked so much by the intensity of our individual suffering as by our willing choice of God's way over our way—no matter what sort of distress we are experiencing or what hardships we are compelled to face. Benner is of the opinion that taking up the cross entails accepting whatever affliction we are subjected to—no matter how great or small—and inviting Christ to walk alongside us as we carry it. It involves meeting the suffering Savior in the crucible of our suffering, and availing ourselves to Jesus in order that we might be touched by *His* grace. Benner concludes that it is through participation in Christ's suffering that modern-day pilgrims are presented the opportunity to put their suffering in perspective and give it meaning, because the end of the way of the Cross is resurrection.[2]

Reflecting on her pain-drenched experiences, Kay recognized that on account of her new orientation to life, she had the spiritual fortitude to meet Jesus in her suffering, because as a suffering Savior He was intimately acquainted with human suffering. And she recognized that He was with her *in* her suffering. This resonates with the words of the ancient prophet, who indicated that our Lord was a man of sorrows and intimately acquainted with grief (see Isa. 53:3). The comforting presence of our suffering Lord encouraged Kay to encounter God in the midst of her suffering, whatever it might be.

Further yet, David G. Benner reminds followers of the Great Galilean that our crosses—once embraced and carried in response to Christ's invitation to follow Him as He followed the divine will of His heavenly Father—become the venue where we meet the divine power that is the *only* agent of our transformation. He indicates that the cross that we take up and carry in response to Jesus's invitation to follow Him becomes the place not only of our death but also of our resurrection.[3]

As previously alluded to, the apostle Paul was someone who was intimately acquainted with suffering of the worst kind. He was also afflicted with what he referred to as a "thorn" in his flesh, which he petitioned God on three separate occasions to remove. God denied Paul's request to remove the "thorn" from his flesh. However, by being compelled to live with his "thorn," Paul discovered that it was in his weakness that he became strong. Paul discovered that it was through the hardships which he was subjected to on account of Christ's sake that he became strong (see 2 Cor. 12:8-10). In like manner as Paul, Kay discovered that by taking up her cross, she was relegated to a place of suffering. But it was in the midst of her suffering that God arrested her and miraculously worked out her transformation. And it was in the midst of suffering that she experienced resurrection possibilities. In like manner as He did for Kay, Jesus promised resurrection possibilities to all those who purpose in their heart to take up their cross and follow Him.

The Bible tells us that God "pitched His tent" (see John 1:14) among us as a Galilean Jew, enfleshed in the garb of humanity, in order to make atonement for the sins of the world. Jesus became intimately acquainted with suffering on account of His ignominious death on Calvary. And He was compelled to pick up His cross and present His heavenly Father the opportunity to meet Him in death and transform His death into resurrection life. In the words of Benner, taking up our individual cross affords suffering to be a place of encountering God. He indicates that despite the intensity of our suffering, God has suffered from it first. And only when we courageously embrace the suffering that can never be avoided are we able to meet the God who is everything and is in everything (see Col. 3:11).[4]

Despite the wrenching experiences that conspired to crack her life open, Kay was endued with life from above that has gone beyond her wildest expectations. Armed with new faith and fortitude, she is thankful for the small epiphanies of daily life; and she is also thankful for the opportunity of being a witness for Christ, ministering to suffering folk in her community who need to hear the good news about the resurrection possibilities that God could accomplish in their broken lives when they surrender their circumstances to His providential care.

Kay currently looks out on life with new eyes and fresh faith. Like Gehazi, God has endowed her with "spiritual optics." As such, she recognizes that God is good even when bad things happen. And every now and then, the realty of God's goodness thrills her soul and brings a smile to her face and a song to her lips, prompting her to lift praise and adoration to God:

I don't feel nowadays tired,

I've come too far from where I started from,

Nobody told me that the road would be easy,

But I don't believe that He brought me this far to leave me.

Like so many of God's children whose circumstances have been transformed by His resurrection possibilities, Kay recognizes that she is truly a walking miracle. As such, she recognizes that praise for the miraculous changes that have been wrought in her life belongs only to Almighty God. Because God did it!

Endnotes

Chapter One: Life Is Sometimes Difficult

1. Scott Peck, *The Road Less Traveled* (New York: Doubleday, 2003), p. 15.

2. Bruce Chilton, *Rabbi Jesus*, (New York: Doubleday, 2002), pp. 61–62.

3. Percy C. Ainsworth, *Weavings*, vol. xxx, no. 4 (Aug/Sep/Oct 2010), p. 26.

4. Saint Augustine, *The City of God*, trans. by Marcus Dods (New York: The Modern Library, 1950).

5. Pierre Teildard de Chardin, *The Divine Milieu* (New York: Harper & Row, 1960), p. 114.

6. Paul Tillich, *Shaking of the Foundations* (New York: Charles Scribner's Sons, 1948), p. 83.

7. C.S. Lewis, *Mere Christianity* (New York: HarperCollins Publishers, 1952), p. 42.

8. John G. Stackhouse Jr., *Can God Be Trusted?* (Downers Grove, Ill.: InterVarsity Press, 2009), p. 62.

9. Saint Augustine, *The City of God.*

10. Jean-Pierre de Caussade, *The Sacrament of the Present Moment,* trans. Kitty Muggeridge (New York: HarperCollins, 1989), p. xvii.

11. David G. Benner, *Opening to God* (Downers Grove, Ill.: InterVarsity Press, 2010), p. 76.

12. Joni Eareckson Tada, *Joni* (Chicago, Ill.: Zondervan Press).

13. Elizabeth Kübler Ross, M.D., *On Death and Dying* (New York: The Macmillan Company, 1969).

14. Ibid., p. 88.

15. Ibid., p. 139.

16. Peter A. Levine, *Healing Trauma: A Pioneering Program for Restoring the Wisdom of Your Body* (Boulder, CO: Sounds True Inc., 1999), p. 3.

17. Jurgen Moltman, *Theology of Hope* (Minneapolis, MN.: Fortress Press, 1991), p. 16.

18. Simone Weil, *Gravity and Grace* (New York: G.P. Putnam's Sons, 1952), p. 87.

19. Lewis, *Mere Christianity,* pp. 17–18.

Chapter Two: Remain Humble During Difficult Times

1. As quoted in C.S. Lewis, *Letters to an American Lady,* ed. Clyde S. Kilby (London: Hodder & Stoughton, 1969), p. 73.

2. Thomas Merton, *A Year With Thomas Merton* (New York: HarperCollins Publishers, 1989), p. 69.

3. Lewis, *Mere Christianity*, p. 164.

4. Thomas Merton, *Life and Holiness* (New York: Image Books Doubleday, 1966), p. 29.

5. Moltman, *Theology of Hope*, p. 19.

Chapter Three: Keep Hope Alive in Difficult Times

1. Howard Thurman, *Jesus and the Disinherited* (Boston: Beacon Press, 1976), p. 21.

2. Viktor Frankl, *Man's Search for Meaning* (New York: Simon & Schuster, 1984), p. 82.

3. Ibid., p. 16.

4. Ibid., p. 113.

5. See *The Ascent of Mount Carmel* in *The Collected Works of St. John of the Cross,* trans. Kiernan Kavanaugh, OCD and Othilio Rodriguez, OCD (Washington, D.C.: ICS Publications, 1973).

6. Nelson Mandela, *Long Walk to Freedom* (Boston, New York, London: Little Brown and Company, 1995), p. 400.

7. C.S. Lewis, *The Problem of Pain* (New York: Harper-Collins, 1996), p. 74.

8. Art Lindsley, *C.S. Lewis's Case for Christ* (Downers Grove, Ill.: InterVarsity Press, 2005), p. 58.

9. Desmond Tutu, *No Future Without Forgiveness* (New York: Image/Doubleday, 1997), p. 164.

10. Frankl, *Man's Search for Meaning*, p. 12.

Chapter Four: Keep Faith Alive in Difficult Times

1. Ainsworth, *Weavings*, p. 26.

2. Judson Cornwall, *Worship as David Lived It* (Shippensburg, PA.: Destiny Image Publishers, 1990), pp. 52–53.

3. Ainsworth, *Weavings*, pp. 23–24.

4. Martin Luther King Jr., *Strength to Love* (Philadelphia: Fortress Press, 1963), p. 134.

5. C.S. Lewis, *Mere Christianity* (New York: Harper-Collins, 1952), p. 80.

6. Paul Tillich, *The New Being* (New York: Charles Scribner's Sons, 1955), p. 121.

Chapter Five: Exercise Patience in Difficult Times

1. Henry Mitchell and Nicholas Lewter, *Soul Theology* (New York: Harper & Rowe, 1986), p. 11.

2. Edward P. Wimberly, *African American Pastoral Care* (Nashville: Abingdon Press, 1991), pp. 11–12.

3. Soren Kierkegaard, *The Sickness Unto Death*, *Kierkegaard's Writings*, Vol. 19 (Princeton University Press, 1980), pp. 29–41.

4. Paul Tillich, *The Courage to Be* (New Haven, Conn.: Yale University Press, 1952).

5. H. Norman Wright, *Resilience* (Ann Arbor, Mich.: Vine Books, 1997), p. 28.

6. Henri J.M. Nouwen, *The Wounded Healer* (New York, Doubleday, 1972).

7. King, *Strength to Love*, p. 72.

Chapter Six: Keep Love Alive in Difficult Times

1. Peck, *The Road Less Traveled*, p. 82.

2. Williston Walker and Richard A. Norris, David Lotz, Robert T. Handy, *A History of the Christian Church* (New York: Scribner, 1985), p. 203.

3. David G. Benner, *Opening to God*, p. 125.

4. Louis Everly, *We Make Bold to Say Our Father*, trans. James Langdale (Grand Rapids, Mich.: Zondervan: Herder & Herder, 1965), p. 11.

5. Andrew Sung Park, *The Wounded Heart of God: The Asian Concept of Han and the Christian Doctrine of Sin* (Nashville, TN: Abingdon Press, 1993), pp. 134–135.

6. Jeremy Taylor, *A Testament of Devotion* (New York: HarperOne, 1941), p. 20.

7. Simone Weil, *Waiting for God* (New York: G.P. Putnam's Sons, 19521), p. 91.

8. Wayne Muller, *Time of Trial* (New York: Bantam Books, 2003), p. 41.

9. King, *Strength to Love*, p. 34.

10. Ibid., p. 34.

11. Ibid.

12. Ibid, p. 33.

13. Peck, *The Road Less Traveled*, p. 83.

14. C.S. Lewis, *Letters to Malcolm: Chiefly on Prayer* (New York: Hartcourt, Brace, & World, 1964), p. 22.

15. Weil, *Gravity and Grace*, p. 111.

16. Tillich, *The Shaking of the Foundation*, p. 156.

Chapter Seven: Turn Difficulties Into Dividends

1. C.S. Lewis, *The Problem of Pain*, p. 123.

2. Philip Yancey, *Where Is God When It Hurts?*

3. Simone Weil, *Waiting for God*, p. 210.

4. C.S. Lewis, *The Problem of Pain*, p. 47.

5. Saint Augustine, *The Confessions of Saint Augustine*, trans, John K. Ryan (Garden City, NY: Doubleday Image Books, 1960), I.I.I., p. 43.

6. Soren Kierkegaard, *Works of Love* (New York: Harper & Row, 1962), p. 93.

7. C.S. Lewis, *The Complete C.S. Lewis: Counting the Cost* (San Francisco: HarperSanFrancisco, 2002), p. 162.

8. Lewis, *The Problem of Pain*, p. 41.

9. John Mogabgab, *Weavings*, vol. vii, no. 3 (May/June 2002), p. 2.

Chapter Eight: Practice Prayer in Difficult Times

1. *The Art of Prayer*, comp. Igumen Chariton of Valamo, trans. E. Kadloubovsky and E.M. Palmer, ed. and intro. Timothy Ware (London: Faber & Faber, 1966), p. 51.

2. Dallas Willard, *The Divine Conspiracy: Rediscovering Our Hidden Life in God* (San Francisco: Harper-SanFrancisco, 1998), p. 194.

3. Ibid., p. 21.

4. Henri Nouwen, *The Wounded Healer*, p. 17.

5. Dietrich Bonhoffer, *Meditating on the Word*, trans. David Mcl. Gracie (Cambridge, MA.: Cowley, 1986), p. 31.

6. John of the Cross, *Dark Night of the Soul*, (New York: Image, 1959).

7. Percy C. Ainsworth, *Weavings, Petitions and Communication*, vol. xxii, no. 4 (July/August 2001), p. 35.

8. Gerrit Scott Dawson, "Prayer in the Triune Life," *Weavings*, vol. xvii, no. 3 (May/June 2002), pp. 13–14.

9. Dawson, "Prayer in the Triune Life," p. 14.

Chapter Nine: Utilize Scripture As a Guide for Living During Difficult Times

1. Peter Toon, *The Art of Meditating on Scripture* (Grand Rapids, Mich.: Zondervan, 1993), p. 74.

Chapter Ten: God Did It

1. Francis A. Schaeffer, *The God Who Is There* (Downers Grove, Ill.: Intervarsity Press, 1968).

2. David G. Benner, *Desiring God's Will* (Downers Grove, Ill.: IVP Books, 2005), p. 96.

3. Ibid., p. 99.

4. Ibid., p. 101.

About Leary E. Bonnett

Leary E. Bonnett is an ordained minister. He earned a Bachelor of Arts Degree in economics from Queens College of The City University of New York, a Master of Human Resources from Webster University in St. Louis, Missouri, a Master of Divinity from New York Theological Seminary, and a Doctor of Ministry from United Theological Seminary in Dayton, Ohio. He is an adjunct professor at New York Theological Seminary.

Dr. Bonnett has ministered to audiences in Africa, Europe, and South America, to name a few. He is the founder of Silence the Guns, a not for profit organization seeking to address the proliferation of gun violence in America. He is currently pursuing studies in the area of Clinical Pastoral Education (CPE) with the Catholic Archdiocese of New York. Dr. Bonnett is a veteran of the United Sates Army in which he served two years as a Combat Medic, and nine years as a Medical Services Officer. He separated from the armed services with the rank of Major.

IN THE RIGHT HANDS, THIS BOOK WILL CHANGE LIVES!

Most of the people who need this message will not be looking for this book. To change their lives, you need to put a copy of this book in their hands.

> *But others (seeds) fell into good ground, and brought forth fruit, some a hundred-fold, some sixty-fold, some thirty-fold* (Matthew 13:8).

Our ministry is constantly seeking methods to find the good ground, the people who need this anointed message to change their lives. Will you help us reach these people?

> *Remember this—a farmer who plants only a few seeds will get a small crop. But the one who plants generously will get a generous crop* (2 Corinthians 9:6).

EXTEND THIS MINISTRY BY SOWING
3 BOOKS, 5 BOOKS, 10 BOOKS, OR MORE TODAY,
AND BECOME A LIFE CHANGER!

Thank you,

Don Nori Sr., Founder
Destiny Image
Since 1982